# PICCADILLY

## The Story of the World's Most Famous Thoroughfare

## BARRY TURNER

MENSCH PUBLISHING

Mensch Publishing
51 Northchurch Road,
London N1 4EE, United Kingdom

First published in Great Britain 2023

A catalogue record for this book is
available from the British Library

ISBN:
978-1-912914-58-6 (paperback)
978-1-912914-59-3 (ebook)

Typeset by Van-garde Imagery, Inc., • van-garde.com

# Contents

# 1

# The Early Days

To go back four hundred years we find that all true Londoners lived within the old City, the square mile now home to the financial sector. As the population increased and commerce expanded, those who could afford to do so reached out to the west to escape what William Petty called 'the fumes, steams and stinks of the whole easterly pile'. While smart houses were built in the Strand alongside the Thames, the father of modern architecture, Inigo Jones, adapted the Italian Renaissance style to create Lincoln's Inn Fields and Covent Garden as residential squares on lines of an Italian piazza.

Meanwhile, what was to become Piccadilly was still virgin territory. Cattle and sheep grazed on green meadows disturbed only by occasional horse riders or the coaches following the rough track to Reading, a bone-shaking distance of some forty miles.

The origin of Piccadilly as a name has long been in dispute. In his *Buildings of England*, Sir Nikolaus Pevsner maintained that the word derived from the Dutch, Pikedillekens, or bits of cloth. The consensus now is that it was Robte Backer or Robert Baker, as he became known, who gave Piccadilly its identity. In 1612 he invested fifty pounds in land 'near the windmill' in what was to become Great Windmill Street. On his newly acquired property, Baker built a house soon dubbed, though not to his liking, Pickadilley Hall, a reference to his speciality, the making of piccadils, a stiff collar or the scalloped edge at the arms of a dress.

Before long, the whole area at the top of Haymarket where farmers came to buy fodder, was known as Piccadilly. The locals worked the land to feed London's burgeoning population, up from 200,000 in 1600 to around 350,000 by mid-century.

Among the landowners who have left their mark was Thomas Pulteney who held the hundred acre St James's farm in the reign of Elizabeth I, at a yearly rent of £7.16 shillings. The Pulteneys were to give their name to one of the first of the Piccadilly hotels that could claim to be more than a coaching inn and to Great Pulteney Street in Soho.

After the English Civil War and Oliver Cromwell's short-lived Commonwealth, a very different Piccadilly began to take shape. The restored monarchy in the person of Charles II found an easy way of rewarding loyalists by doling out parcels of land close to Westminster, the centre of royal power.

One of the first to benefit was Henry Jermyn, First Earl of St Albans, who speculated on laying out St James's Square on the side of Pall Mall to provide town houses for the aristocracy and more modest houses for letting to the professional classes.

On the grandest scale was the project undertaken by Edward Hyde, Earl of Clarendon and Lord Chancellor, in effect, chief minister to Charles II. To build a palace fit for the King's favourite, he chose as his site the open countryside bordering Piccadilly. Between 1664 and 1667, three hundred men were engaged on building what the diarist John Evelyn described as 'the most useful, graceful and magnificent house in England' with gardens covering eight acres.

Unfortunately for Clarendon, no sooner was he ready to move in than his power ran out. He had enemies on all sides. Those who had thrived under Cromwell were naturally averse but he was also harassed by fellow royalists who were jealous of his position, particularly after the marriage of his daughter to James, Duke of York, the King's brother and heir apparent.

In 1665, it was Clarendon who suffered the backlash from the bubonic plague which decimated the old city with its cramped streets and open sewers. The following year, the conspiracy mongers held the Lord Chancellor to blame for the Great Fire which made over 70,000 Londoners homeless.

The odds were even further stacked against Clarendon by his conduct of foreign affairs. A sensible decision to dispose of Dunkirk, a British outpost across the Channel, raised the ire of patriots who were further incensed when the Dutch navy devastated the British fleet at anchor on the River Medway. Loud were the excuses of the 'gentleman captains' whose nautical ignorance was matched by their reluctance to put themselves at risk.

The King took it out on Clarendon. With the consequences of impeachment hanging over him, he fled the country. His mansion was let out until his death in 1674 when it was sold to the Duke of Albemarle. A free spender and hard drinker, Albemarle was in no position to enjoy his acquisition. Instead he got himself appointed governor of Jamaica where he devoted his energies to a hunt for sunken treasure.

Clarendon House was almost a ruin when, according to Evelyn, it was bought by a syndicate 'of rich bankers and mechanics', headed by Sir Thomas Bond. The site was cleared to make way for Bond Street, Dover Street and Albemarle Street, the latter destined to be London's first one-way thoroughfare, running through the centre of what had been Clarendon House.

By then, work had started on a church for Piccadilly. Land had been set aside by the Earl of St Albans but there was a delay in starting work as the favoured architect, Sir Christopher Wren, was too busy erecting city churches to replace those lost in the Great Fire. After the foundation stone for St James's was laid on 3 April 1676 it was another eight years before it opened for worship. Wren was easily forgiven. By common consent, he had created a masterpiece, providing 'a room so capacious as with pews and galleries to hold two thousand persons and all to hear the service and see the preacher'.

Among the first to visit the church, Evelyn gave particular praise to the carvings of Grinling Gibbons, dubbed the 'Michelangelo of Wood'. 'There is no altar anywhere in England,' he wrote, 'nor has there been any abroad, more handsomely adorned.' The font, sanctuary and the organ were all embellished by Gibbons. Hostile criticism was reserved for the steeple, though Wren was hardly to blame. His design, judged to be too expensive, was rejected for a cheaper version drawn up by a local carpenter, a false economy as it turned out since it was not long before it had to be replaced.

The steeple came down and the church all but wrecked in 1940 by a German bomb. While the Gibbons carvings survived under protective covering, St James's remained a roofless shell for seven years.

St James's Piccadilly, consecrated in 1684,
a Christopher Wren masterpiece

There has always been a touch of the unorthodox in the history of St James's. Today its mission is 'to create a space where people of any faith or none can question and discover the sacred life through openness, struggle, laughter and prayer.'

Burials include auctioneer James Christie who founded nearby Christie's and caricaturist James Gillray and Dutch artists Willem van de Velde, Elder and Younger. A memorial to the botanical artist Mary Delaney records how the niece of Lord Lansdowne married Patrick Delaney, a poor Irish priest, the illegitimate son of a servant girl. For unusual weddings, the prize must go to the explorer Sir Samuel Baker who, in 1865, married a young woman he had bought at a Turkish slave auction.

Of all the Piccadilly aristocrats who have worshipped at St James's, the most endearingly eccentric was the Duke of Cambridge, brother of George IV. The Duke was given to speaking his thoughts in a loud bellow and on Sundays could be heard giving a running commentary on the sermon. When the parson concluded with, 'Let us pray', the Duke would raise his voice to declare graciously, 'By all means, my dear fellow, by all means.' On one occasion, after listening attentively to the reading of the Commandments, he added to the seventh, 'No, no; it was my brother Ernest who broke that one.'

Burlington House, better known today as the Royal Academy of Arts, was one of the earliest grand houses to be built on the north side of Piccadilly. The mansion was yet to be finished when it was bought by the 1st Earl of Burlington in 1667. It was the 3rd Earl, with his passion for architecture and landscaping, who gave Burlington House its distinctive appearance. This was inspired by the northern Italian Renaissance architect, Andrea Palladio, who followed the clean classical lines of Greek and Roman architecture. Such was Burlington's devotion to Palladio and such was his influence on contemporary taste, that by the mid-eighteenth century, the Palladian style ruled supreme over architectural practice.

The Royal Academy, originally the home of
the Earls of Burlington

Burlington faced his house with stone, replacing the red brick favoured by the first Earl, and erected a magnificent colonnade. Though greatly admired, it was hidden from Piccadilly by what was said to be 'the most expensive wall in England' though 'wonderfully proportioned to the length'.

Described by Horace Walpole as 'the Apollo of the Arts', Burlington turned his home into something of an artists' commune. Of the resident guests, George Frederic Handel wrote three of his operas here while frequent visitors included the poet

nder Pope and John Gay of *The Beggars' Opera*
ᴮurlington's credit that he recognised Gay's tal-
ᴴeme of *The Beggars' Opera*, that while rich and
poor were equally susceptible to vice, it was the poor who reaped
the punishment, did not go down well in polite society.

It was Lord George Cavendish, a later Earl of Burlington, the
first by a second creation (the history of the British aristocracy
is not easily disentangled) who built the Burlington Arcade, the
first enclosed shopping street in London, 'a covered promenade
with shops on either side for the sale of jewellery and fancy ob-
jects of fashionable demand'. He was motivated, it was said, by a
desire to serve the public and 'to give employment to industrious
females', presumably as shop assistants. The popular assumption
was that the Arcade prevented passers-by from throwing rubbish
into his garden. Employed to keep order, livered beadles were re-
cruited from Lord George's regiment, the 10th Hussars. The rules
they were expected to enforce included no whistling, running,
playing musical instruments or the opening of umbrellas. The
Arcade opened for business in 1819 and has remained fashionable ever since, its appeal enhanced recently by a multi-million
pound facelift.

Burlington House was sold to the government in 1854 as a
prospective site for a National Gallery. When it was instead decided to start afresh with a National Gallery in Trafalgar Square,
Burlington House was leased to the Royal Academy. The 'most
expensive wall in England' was demolished and a new front was
added to accommodate such learned institutions as the Geological

Society, the Society of Antiquaries and the Royal Astronomical Society.

Not long into the eighteenth century the area around Piccadilly was finding favour with the *nouveau riche*, whose wealth was founded on business and the professions. As early as 1708 *A New View of London* described Albemarle Street as 'a Street of excellent new Building inhabited by Persons of Quality between the Fields and Portugal Street', while Dover Street was 'a street of very good Buildings, mostly inhabited by Gentry'.

Linking into Piccadilly, Mayfair was no longer the site of a riotous spring fair. In its glory days, it covered thirteen acres of itinerant traders and promoters of bare-knuckle prize fighting, bull and bear baiting and freak shows. In their place came three magnificent squares starting with Hanover Square, laid out after 1714 with spacious houses inhabited by 'persons of distinction'. The Hanover Square Rooms were famed for their concerts. J.S. Bach, Haydn, Paganini and Liszt all performed there.

Berkeley Square, carved out of fields beyond the garden of Berkeley (later Devonshire) House, took shape after 1737 at about the same time as Grosvenor Square, where the Duchess of Kendal, George I's mistress, was among the earliest residents. Their daughter, Petronilla Melusina married the 4th Earl of Chesterfield who built a house on the north side of Curzon Street, facing Hyde Park. His friends teased him for choosing such a way out place to live, telling him that he had no right to call his new home a town house since it was so far from the city centre. Chesterfield himself quipped that with few friends willing to take the trouble to call on him, he would need a dog to keep him company.

Chesterfield was an eccentric with a sense of the ridiculous. In his picture gallery where hung the portraits of his ancestors, he extended the lineage of the Stanhope family name to include Adam de Stanhope and Eve de Stanhope. Unable to take himself or the royal court too seriously and having missed out on a political career, except for a brief period as Lord Lieutenant of Ireland, Chesterfield retired into private life at the age of fifty-four. He is now best remembered for the letters he wrote to his son, Philip Stanhope, handing out advice which for the most part the recipient rejected. Many of Chesterfield's pithy sayings still strike a chord. How right he was to observe that 'advice is seldom welcome and those who need it most always like it least'. Nor was he far from the truth when he claimed that 'without some dissimulation no business can be carried on at all'. The opinion that runs throughout the letters is nowhere better demonstrated than in Chesterfield's view of sex.

*The pleasure is momentary, the position ridiculous and the expense damnable.*

Few of his contemporaries, male or female, agreed with him except, possibly, about the expense.

Chesterfield House was pulled down in 1937 to meet the demand for luxury flats.

Built early in the reign of George III, Gloucester House at 137 Piccadilly gained distinction as the first exhibition site for the Elgin Marbles. Originally attached to the Parthenon in Athens, the Marbles were shipped to Britain by Thomas Bruce, 7th Earl of Elgin, British ambassador in Constantinople when Greece was under Turkish rule. So began an international dispute over ownership that has still to be resolved.

Elgin claimed to have acquired the statuary legitimately, having successfully negotiated with the Sultan for its removal. Moreover, it was claimed, had the Marbles stayed at the Acropolis they might well have ended up as building material, their value unrecognised by the Turkish occupiers. Recent evidence suggests that Turkish sensitivities were not as blunted as Elgin made out.

With possession being nine tenths of the law, particularly when the aristocracy was involved, Elgin was able to sell the Marbles to the British government. While contributing to the cost of his divorce, he complained that the sum raised fell short of the money he had spent on acquiring and shipping the Marbles. Handed over to the British Museum in 1816, they are now displayed in the purpose-built Duveen Gallery with their future frequently under negotiation.

As for Gloucester House, it was subsequently occupied by two royal dukes – the Duke of Gloucester from 1816 to 1834 and the Duke of Cambridge to 1904 when it was pulled down to make way for a block of luxury flats and, as from 1971, the Hard Rock Café.

Despite the infusions of old and new money, Piccadilly in the late eighteenth century retained much of its rakish character. Hyde Park Corner was judged to be 'a most wretched place'. According to the German-born travel writer Max Schlesinger:

> *There were a great many taverns whose fame was none of the best; and, on review days, the soldiers from the neigh-*

*bouring barracks sat in front of the houses on wooden
benches, whilst their hair was being powdered, and their
pig-tails tied up. During this interesting operation, they
laughed and joked with the maid-servants who passed that
way. As a natural consequence of these proceedings, the
quarter was avoided by the respectable classes.*

This was putting it mildly. Highwaymen and footpads preyed on the unwary. After nightfall, few dared to walk alone from Kensington to the more salubrious parts of Piccadilly. At Hyde Park corner, a bell was rung at seven and at nine o'clock as a call to those who sought safety in numbers.

Piccadilly and prostitution have had a long association. As early as 1606, an ordinance to lop the hedges and clear out the ditches was judged to be urgent because, 'Thieves and harlots shelter there to the destruction of the King's subjects in winter time and in summer time all the harlots continue to be there.' Neither thieves nor harlots were deterred.

Throughout the eighteenth century, foreign visitors to London were shocked by the swarm of 'street girls, well got-up and well-dressed, displaying their attractions'. This was Friedrich Wilhelm von Schutz, whose *Letters from London* was published in Hamburg in 1792. Von Schutz concluded, 'no place in the world can be compared with London for wantonness'.

While suspect figures were bandied about by campaigners for a crackdown (estimates of up to 50,000 prostitutes active in London, this of a population of one million, are hard to credit) it was nonetheless true that the wages of sin were a great attraction to those on the breadline. If it came to a choice, a career in the streets was less dangerous than the workshop, less onerous than domestic service and paid better than both. A young and attractive prostitute could earn up to £400 a year, more than twice the pay of a skilled craftsman. The risks were contracting syphilis or gonorrhoea (a risk shared by their clients) and the occasional appearance before a magistrate for soliciting which, unlike prostitution as such, was illegal.

Across the board, sensitivity to the human condition was at a low ebb. In clear sight of some of Piccadilly's finest houses was the track that led to Tyburn. Public hangings were frequent under Georgian rule. Thirty-three new capital offences were created under George III. With little or no debate, Parliament raised the number of capital crimes from around fifty at the start of the Georgian period to about 200 at the end. A pick-pocket could be hanged for stealing 12 pence. It was not until 1783 that Tyburn ceased to be a place of execution.

But whatever its unsavoury features, Piccadilly remained the first choice for those who could afford palatial homes. One of the grandest was built for the Devonshire family on a site opposite of what is now the Ritz Hotel. The architect was William Kent, a protégé of the Earl of Burlington. The 'plain severity' of the Palladian exterior was not to everyone's taste. Topographer James Ralph, a devotee of traditional Gothic, compared the house to an East India Company warehouse, adding sniffily, 'both are equally deserving of praise'. Hidden from Piccadilly strollers by a high brick wall, 'cheerless and unsociable by day and terrible by night', said a critic, the wall also blocked out the view from the house of

Green Park, then known as Upper St James's Park, with its grazing cattle and deer, not to mention more nefarious activities.

Where Kent could not be faulted was in his design for the state apartments, unrivalled in their ornate magnificence.

*A crowd of 1,200 could easily sweep through the house during a ball, a remarkable contrast to some great houses where the crush could lift a person off his feet and carry him from room to room. Guests entered the house by an outer staircase which took them directly to the first floor. Inside was a hall two storeys high – flanked on either side by two drawing rooms of identical size. Beyond the hall was another, even larger drawing room, several anterooms and the dining room. Some of the finest paintings in England adorned the walls, including Rembrandt's Old Man in Turkish Dress, and Poussin's Et in Arcadia Ego.*

Completed around 1740, Devonshire House came into the possession of the 4th Duke shortly after the death from smallpox of his young wife, Charlotte Cavendish. The daughter and sole heir of the 3rd Earl of Burlington, Charlotte made the enormously wealthy Devonshires richer still by handing down Chiswick House in London, Londesborough Hall and Bolton Abbey, both in Yorkshire, Lismore Castle in County Waterford in Ireland and Burlington House in Piccadilly.

With more than enough property to accommodate the Duke, Devonshire House was virtually unoccupied until 1774 when William, the 5th in succession, married the 17-year-old

Georgiana Spencer, eldest daughter of Earl Spencer. Landed with a boring and gauche husband who favoured his drinking cronies to the company of his wife, Georgiana was left to her own devices. This suited her admirably. A buoyant and independent spirit with a talent for holding her own in conversation with whomever she happened to meet, the young Duchess was on every society invitation list. A few weeks after her arrival in London, Horace Walpole was full of praise for this 'lovely girl, natural and full of grace'. Her success was achieved 'without being a beauty; but her youth, figure, flowing good nature, sense and lively modesty ... made her a phenomenon'.

Georgiana came quickly to understand the liberties and limitations of her privileged position. The ruling class made few concessions to domestic convention. Open marriages were commonplace. The trend had been set by Charles II, 'the merry monarch', who sired twelve children by various mistresses. While it was *de rigueur* for rich husbands to indulge in extra-marital affairs, their wives were equally at liberty to share their favours. Clever women read the same books as men, laughed at the same bawdy jokes and talked politics on an equal footing. Women hunted and shot, played cricket and rowed. 'They do whatever they please,' observed the Italian traveller, Gemelli Careri, 'and do so generally wearing the breeches ... that it has now become a proverb that England is the hell of horses and the paradise of women; and if there were a bridge from the island to the continent, all the women in Europe would run thither.'

Georgiana, Duchess of Devonshire, the social
and political superstar of Georgian England

This is not to say that women were treated as equals.
Chesterfield's view of women as 'only children of larger growth'
was generally acknowledged by both sexes.

But if women of wealth and breeding could not expect to rise
to the political heights they could, and did, advance the interests
of the men in their lives. Georgiana was of this ilk. A star of the
gossip mongers with her magnificent receptions at Devonshire

House she devoted her talents to promoting the Whigs, the political alliance that championed parliament at the expense of the royal prerogative exercised by George III.

As the leading exponent of Whiggism, Charles James Fox was always a welcome guest at Devonshire House where his parliamentary triumphs were celebrated in style, no expense spared. Handsome in his youth, the mature Fox was paunchy and untidy with a swarthy skin and black, shaggy eyebrows. A hard-drinking gambler who had frittered away the family fortune, he was constantly in debt. But all was forgiven of a great orator and dazzling conversationalist. 'No public man has been so loved by his associates.'

But while Fox campaigned for the abolition of the slave trade, argued for the reform of the administration of India by the corrupt and incompetent East India Company, supported American independence and subscribed to the ideals of the French Revolution, he and his reviled Tory opponents had much in common. Both were led by powerful families who put their own interests before all else. Condemning the corruption at Court, Fox was not above accepting well paid sinecures.

While the Tories gave comfort to the King, his heir, the Prince of Wales, allied himself to the Whigs who took his side in the increasingly acrimonious relations between father and son. Inevitably, there were rumours of an affair between the Prince and Georgiana. Beyond gossip there was little supporting evidence but they were close enough for her to be a calming influence. Not that it did much good. Handsome as a young man, the Prince had excellent taste in all except his fondness for rakish companions. He fell in love very easily. At age sixteen he was said to have seduced one of the Queen's maids of honour. His passionate affair with an actress, Mary Robinson, cost him dearly when she had to be paid off. But he failed to learn from his experience. Always partial to mature ladies of full figure, he fell madly in love with Marie Fitzherbert, a wealthy widow six years older than her pursuer. Enormously rich after the death of her second husband, Marie was not immune to royal flattery. But she was also a devout Catholic who would not countenance an intimate relationship outside marriage. Desperate to fulfil what was now his only aim in life, the Prince defied the King and constitution by persuading an Anglican person to conduct a wedding ceremony that, if recognised, would cut him out of the succession. The law was clear on this point. Both the Act of Settlement and the Royal Marriages Act ruled that no-one who married a Catholic could accede to the throne.

Fox did his best to defend the Prince accusing his critics in the House of Commons of 'miserable calumnies' while privately admitting that the Prince had taken a 'very desperate step'. Both Fox and, eventually, the Prince managed to persuade themselves that the marriage had never happened.

1783 was the year in which the American colonies gained their independence and William Pitt, at the tender age of 24, became prime minister. Loyal to the King, he also attracted moderate reformers who disliked Fox and his roughshod political tactics. But having taken over from a shaky coalition led by the Duke of Portland (husband of Dorothy Cavendish, the Duke of Devonshire's sister) in which Fox had been foreign minister, Pitt could only secure his position by a winning a majority in a general election. This took place in March 1784. The closest fought campaign was in Westminster, one of the country's largest constituencies embracing St James's, Piccadilly and Soho. Two seats were in contention. Since there could be no doubt that Admiral Lord Hood, a naval hero, would top the poll, the battle was for the second seat with Fox against Sir Cecil Wray, an old political hand and formidable advocate for the Tory royalists.

Since the twelve thousand electors had forty days over which they could register their choice, the opportunities for bribery and intimidation was legion. Georgiana was in the thick of it. Wild stories circulated of kisses bestowed on the most unlikely recipients. 'She is in the street, they tell me almost every day', wrote Mrs Boscawen to Lady Chatham, 'And this is her sole employment from morning till night. She gets out of her carriage and walks into alleys ... [with] many blackguards in her suit.' Earl Temple was of the opinion that the Duchess had 'heard more plain English of the grossest sort that ever fell ... to any lady of her rank'.

Georgiana's mother, Lady Spencer, begged her daughter to withdraw before she disgraced herself and her family. Georgiana held to her cause while denying strenuously that she was offending propriety. There was no truth, she said, in the rumour that she had kissed a butcher.

A narrow victory for Fox was immediately challenged. (It was eight months before Wray finally conceded.) But this did not dampen the celebrations. Fox was carried in triumphal procession along Piccadilly to Devonshire House. A Falstaffian figure, relishing the adoration of the crowd, he was preceded by twenty-four horsemen, dressed in the Whig colours of blue and buff. The drinks flowed freely as the resplendent Georgiana shared the glory by giving the party of a lifetime. Never again would Devonshire House see such abandon.

The Duke was noticeable by his absence. He had other matters to occupy him. Though occasionally appearing together to keep up appearances, he and Georgiana led separate lives.

Something of the double standards of the Devonshire set was given wide circulation by Richard Brinsley Sheridan, playwright, womaniser and scrounger, whose ear for gossip inspired *School for Scandal*. As a central character in the comedy, Lady Teazle was assumed to be a lampoon of Georgiana. It was a connection the Duchess resented but there was little she could do. Changing her behaviour was not an option.

The Duke was not entirely immune to scandal. While he fathered two illegitimate children, his anger showed when Georgiana's affair with the 23-year-old future prime minister, Charles Grey, produced a daughter. Resenting a young rival, the Duke delivered an ultimatum. Georgiana could keep the baby and live with Grey or accept a formal separation. This raised the prospect of never again seeing her other children, including her one-year-old son. Georgiana accepted the inevitable.

But if the relationship between Georgiana and her husband ended acrimoniously it had less to do with her infidelities as with the massive debts she mounted up as an inveterate gambler. Exiled to France, Georgiana returned home when war broke out in 1793. But the great days were long gone. She died in 1806.

As for Devonshire House, its sad fate comes later in the Piccadilly story.

# 2
# Lady M

When Georgiana was at the height of her powers, she was close to another reigning hostess of Piccadilly. Elizabeth Lamb, Viscountess Melbourne, is said to have been 'one of the most remarkable women of her age'. With beauty, brains and inexhaustible energy, she devoted her life to politics and social advancement with all that they had to offer. She and Georgiana were two of a kind.

The daughter of an old Yorkshire county family, Elizabeth was born to wealth which increased substantially when, at the age of seventeen, she married Sir Peniston Lamb, owner of Brocket Hall, a Palladian mansion on the river Lea in Hertfordshire and Melbourne Hall in Derbyshire. They also had a town house, 28 Sackville Street, just off Piccadilly.

In May 1769, Elizabeth or Betsy as she was known to the family, had her first child, a boy who was baptised at St James's, Piccadilly. Having established her marital credentials, Elizabeth turned her mind to creating a social and political base from which she could mount her all-absorbing campaign to secure a peerage for her husband. The first requirement was a large house for entertaining and to assert her family's place in the aristocratic pecking order. The site chosen was on Piccadilly just round the corner from Sackville Street, close to Burlington House. Aiming for the best, Sir William Chambers, joint architect to the King, was commissioned to carry out the work. The budget was flexible.

Melbourne House began to take shape in the early 1770s. Building was proceeding 'very briskly' reported Chambers as he outlined his plans for magnificent reception rooms overlooking the garden to the rear of the house.

Lady Melbourne, a leading hostess, free with her favours, and mother of future prime minister, Lord Melbourne

For the interior, the services were engaged of Giovanni Cipriani, the fashionable Italian painter and engraver. Favouring rich colours and *trompe l'oeil* three dimensional images, Cipriani set to painting the moulded ceiling of the fifty-two-foot-long saloon where the future Lady Melbourne was to hold her glittering receptions. Below the saloon and of the same dimensions was the dining room with its panels of 'green on a white ground' with surrounds of 'pale buff'. At one end of the room a large bay window gave a panoramic view of the garden. At the opposite end stood a colonnade of Ionic columns. So much was eye-catchingly impressive, if perhaps a little too flamboyant.

The furnishing was equally extravagant. Gracing the dining room, a sideboard of polished inlaid wood by Thomas Chippendale was the most expensive piece of furniture to come out of his workshop. It was later bought by the Sitwell family for Renishaw Hall in Derbyshire where it is known as the Renishaw commode. Peniston fretted at the invoices delivered to Brocket Hall but otherwise was content for his wife to handle the everyday management while he gave himself to rural pursuits.

In early 1774, the Melbournes gave two concerts to celebrate moving into their new home. But there was still much to be done. As late as November, Peniston was writing to Chambers looking for assurance that the workmen would be out of the house by the New Year, with all the scaffolding removed from the gateway and the dirt cleaned away.

Elizabeth did not allow such details to cramp her style. Her receptions, in the Whig interest, rivalled those of her friend, Georgiana, Duchess of Devonshire. Her love life was equally vigorous. With her natural beauty and winning personality, she attracted a bevy of male admirers several of whom found their way into her bed. But she did what she regarded as her duty by her husband, giving birth to six children, albeit of doubtful paternity, and making their home an assembly of all the talents.

Melbourne contrived to pay whatever bills fell on to his desk while finding comfort in the embrace of an actress, Mrs Baddeley, whose maintenance proved to be as expensive as that of his wife. Attempts to economise left money owing to William Chambers. Ten years after the completion of Melbourne House his account was still £3,000 short. He had to make do with the security of a bond on which the interest was two years in arrears. In fairness to Melbourne, the final cost of construction, put at £100,000, was way ahead of the original estimates though closer attention to the accounts might have saved him embarrassment.

Spotting the paternal responsibility for Elizabeth's children was an obsession with journalists and gossip mongers. Of long running interest was the question of who fathered William, the second eldest of Elizabeth's offspring, who was destined to be Queen Victoria's first prime minister and close confidant. The consensus favoured the 3rd Earl of Egremont, whose Palladian town house was 94 Piccadilly. Built around 1760 on the site of an inn facing Green Park, Egremont House (later Cambridge House) was originally known as 'the last home in Piccadilly' since for a time it was the most westerly of all the great houses. The first occupant, the 2nd Earl, died of apoplexy in the home he had so recently created, the victim, it was said, of gluttony. A few days before his death he announced, 'I have three more turtle dinners to come. If I survive the last of them, I shall be immortal.' He didn't and he wasn't.

As his son and successor, the 3rd Earl was of more sophisticated bent. A patron of the arts, he was one of the earliest to recognise the genius of J.M.W. Turner, forerunner of impressionism. Turner was a welcome guest at Petworth, the Sussex county seat of the Egremonts. He demanded and was given total seclusion. In a studio fitted up to his specifications where admission was granted only by a pre-arranged tap on the door. His patron was not exempt from the rule. The reward was a collection of Turner's paintings, still held at Petworth, latterly in the care of the National Trust.

Egremont's largesse extended to less talented artists, now scarcely remembered, and he gave away to charity about a quarter of his total income. Even then there was enough left over for him to indulge his passion for horse racing. His stable celebrated winning both the Derby and the Oaks, the latter no fewer than five times.

Of all his leisure pursuits, sex was high on the list. Handsome, amusing and enormously rich, he attracted a succession of mistresses who provided him with an extended family of impressive size. Countess Spencer, a fiercely disapproving critic of Piccadilly lifestyle, confidently asserted that Egremont had at least forty-three children living with their mothers at Petworth, where they 'make scenes worthy of Billingsgate or a Mad House'.

Egremont was besotted by Elizabeth. How could it have been otherwise with his roving eye ever on the lookout for beauty combined with a sharp intelligence and zest for life. But assuming that Egremont was William's father (the dark brown hair and flashing eyes were a giveaway) there was never any question of Elizabeth and her lover making a life together. Both had other fish to fry.

Still in pursuit of a peerage for her husband, an honour she could share as Lady Melbourne, Elizabeth encouraged the romantic advances of George, Prince of Wales. When in May 1782, Elizabeth gave birth to a third son, gossip credited George with a notable conquest. Elizabeth strenuously denied the rumour though it did not pass notice that she made no pretence that her husband was responsible for the conception.

Sexual favours required a payback. Having reached his twenty-first birthday, the Prince was now in a position to reward his friends. The *London Gazette* for 1783 announced the appointment of Lord Melbourne as a Gentleman of the Bedchamber, a position of minimal responsibility but one that came with a Viscountcy, albeit an Irish peerage. It was not quite good enough for Elizabeth who had expected to join the English nobility but at a time when in total there were fewer than two hundred peers of the realm, she had to settle for what she could get.

By July 1784, when a fourth son was born, there could be no doubt that the Prince of Wales was responsible. If the shock of light red hair was not evidence enough, naming the baby George removed all doubts. Elizabeth's pregnancy held her back from engaging in the 1784 Westminster election with quite the same dedication as Georgiana but in her support for Fox, she was 'no less enthusiastic' while at Melbourne House, the Whig leaders were to be found plotting their tactics against the Tory majority in Parliament.

If the Prince of Wales was always a welcome guest at Melbourne House, so too was his younger brother, Frederick Duke of York, who was on much better terms with his father, George III. Elizabeth believed in keeping her options open. It turned out to be a wise policy. When the Melbourne money began to run out (as late as 1789, the debt to Sir William Chambers had to be covered by a mortgage on the Piccadilly house) the Duke of York came up with an offer that could not be refused. Having decided that Melbourne House was where he most wanted to live, a complicated financial deal involving an exchange of properties allowed for the Duke to move to Piccadilly while the Melbournes decamped to Whitehall to a new classical residence later to be known as Dover House and later still as the Scottish Office. There they remained until 1830.

Meanwhile, in 1815, Lord Melbourne was raised to the English peerage with a seat in the House of Lords. Elizabeth died three years later, aged 67. Her son William, 2nd Lord Melbourne, provided a fitting epitaph.

> *My mother was a most remarkable woman, not merely clever and engaging but the most sagacious woman I knew. She kept me straight as long as she lived ... A remarkable woman, and devoted mother, and excellent wife – but not chaste, not chaste.*

Renaming Melbourne House as York House, the 30-year-old Duke of York was in his element. With an insatiable appetite for the good things in life, Piccadilly was for him the near perfect environment.

But this affable, overweight and self-indulgent prince was not allowed to give himself up entirely to a life of pleasure. George III had determined on a military career for his favourite son, an objective achieved by the simple procedure of gazetting him colonel in 1780, major general in 1782 and lieutenant general in 1784. Eleven years later, he was promoted to field marshal and given command of the British army, this at a critical stage in the war with France. Displaying no talent as a field commander and too easily diverted from his duties by the gambling table, he took the blame for setbacks in the campaign to frustrate Napoleon's ambitions to dominate Europe.

His lowest point came in 1809 when it was revealed that his former mistress, the flamboyant Mrs Mary Anne Clarke, had been accepting money from officers in return for using her influence with the Duke to gain them promotion. A Parliamentary inquiry cleared the Duke of corruption but not before a cross examination of Mary Clarke had laid bare his extravagance on her behalf, running to an annual allowance of £1,000 with twenty servants and two coaches for personal use.

The scandal all but ended the Duke's military career but his legacy is not entirely without merit. Though parodied as the Grand Old Duke of York who had no idea what to do with ten thousand men except to march them up a hill then march them down again, he was smart enough to realise that his tactical deficiencies were part of a wider problem, a consequence of the poor state of the army and the lack of professionalism in the higher ranks.

Appearances were all. An example of the peculiar order of priorities adopted by commissioned officers was six thousand tons of flour were bought each year for the powdering of army wigs. It was to the Duke's credit that he embarked on wholesale reforms that brought the military to an unprecedented level of efficiency. He founded the Royal Military College, raised the pay of ordinary servicemen, improved standards of medical treatment and did away with barbaric living conditions.

His memorial column, 124 feet high, in Waterloo Place testifies as much to the respect of his fellow soldiers as to their deference to royalty. But if the Duke's reputation passed muster with the comrades in arms, he was held in lower regard by those to whom he owed money. By 1800, saddled with gambling debts he had no immediate prospect of paying off, he put on a show of economy (it didn't last) by deciding to sell off his house in Piccadilly

In Thomas Malton's *Picturesque Tour through London and Westminster*, published in 1792, a radical plan was mooted for 'building a street of handsome houses on the gardens (of York House) in a direct line with Savile Row'. This would call for the demolition of York House.

The prime movers were the architect Henry Holland, a builder's son who had married the daughter of landscape designer 'Capability' Brown, Thomas Coutts, head of Coutts Bank and financial adviser to the great and good, and Alexander Copland, a builder or, more accurately, a property developer noted for constructing large public buildings such as barracks and military hospitals on budget and on time. After the Duke agreed to a long lease, Coutts put up the money.

But there was a hitch. Overlooking Burlington House, the new residences were judged to be an invasion of privacy. Copland came up with an alternative plan. Having settled with the Duke for the outright purchase of the site with payments to be made in instalments, a prospectus announced 'large additions' to the mansion and 'such alterations as are necessary to open the whole as a magnificent and convenient hotel'.

The concept was novel at the turn of the century. While modest hotels and lodgings could be found in or around Piccadilly, wealthy visitors had higher expectations. To fill the gap in the market, the Royal York Hotel was set to open in the summer of 1803. Then, for reasons unknown though possibly to minimise the financial risk, the Copland-led syndicate decided that the converted buildings were to be sold as 'separate lots of apartments'. While the central structure was to be retained, to the rear two long blocks of apartments, three storeys high running the full length of the garden were to be divided by a paved covered walk over an equidistant underground corridor for deliveries and for servants going about their business.

At the far end of the garden, two more blocks were planned with a porter's lodge guarding the northern entrance from Vigo Street. The Piccadilly frontage was marked out for four shops occupied by a gold and silver lace manufacturers, a druggist, a pastry cook and fruiterer and a linen designer. The shop windows were framed by six eagles, modelled in Coade stone which appeared to support the balconies above on their outstretched wings. The downside to the conversion was the loss of the great flying staircase in the entrance hall described by Sir John Soane as 'worthy of being placed in competition with the finest productions of Italy'.

With the overall feel of an Oxbridge college, the appeal was to single males (no women) whether committed bachelors or to married men living separate lives. The collective name for what was to be the smartest bachelor address in town was The Albany (the Duke of York was also Duke of Albany) though the definite article was dropped early in the twentieth century to make the place sound less like a public house.

Since it was assumed that residents would eat out, no kitchens were incorporated but there was to be a restaurant and hot and cold baths were promised. After seven years of losing money, the restaurant closed in 1810; the baths were never built.

With apartments offered on 99-year leases on conditions laid down by elected trustees, short stays were not anticipated. In the event, provisions for sub-letting allowed for occupation for a year or two, an option that became increasingly popular.

Albany, originally the home of Lady Melbourne, was converted into bachelor apartments and remains today one of the smartest addresses in London

There was flexibility too in the 'no business rule'. When Robert Smirke succeeded Henry Holland as the consulting architect, he was permitted to live and work in Albany. With an initial slow take up (by 1804 only ten apartments were occupied) the business rule was further adjusted to accommodate the famous Harry Angelo and his fencing school. He shared courtyard chambers with Gentleman John Jackson, the prize fighter who gave lessons in pugilism. That he was at the top of his profession was beyond question. He could lift ten-and-a quarter hundredweight and sign his name with an eighty-four pound weight tied to his little finger. He was heavyweight champion of England for eight years. After breaking a leg in a fight that caused him to have a fall, he offered to finish the contest 'tied to a chair'.

Albany and its residents are a recurring feature in the story of Piccadilly but, for now, let us give credit to Alexander Copland as the originator of London's first apartment block, pre-dating Queen Anne Mansions in Victoria by over fifty years.

# 3
# High Life, Low Life

The concentration of wealth in Piccadilly pointed up the contrasts in Georgian society, not simply between rich and poor but between conflicting standards that made for a brutish society within a civilised framework. Cruel sports such as cock fighting and bear baiting were popular while public executions attracted huge crowds. Abject poverty with women and children starving in the streets was tolerated as part of the natural order.

Next to sex, the great obsession of the rich was with gambling. By the late eighteenth century, from end to end in Piccadilly, thousands of pounds changed hands every evening. What today are prestigious clubs such as Whites, Brooks's and Boodle's were thinly disguised casinos. Attendance at such as the Coventry House Club at 106 Piccadilly was promoted by the offer of free suppers. Horace Walpole said of Brooks's that it was a place 'where a thousand meadows and cornfields were staked at every throw'. It was at Brooks's that the sandwich, pieces of salt beef between two slices of toast, was popularised by the eponymous Earl who was ill-disposed to interrupt his gambling for supper.

Around 1805, 81 Piccadilly, an unpretentious house at the corner of Bolton Street, took the name of Watier's. It was inspired by the Prince Regent (later George IV) who invited his chef, Jean Baptiste Watier, to set up a dinner club where gamblers could enjoy a meal that departed from 'the eternal joints of beef steaks and boiled fowl with oyster sauce and an apple tart'. The club was popular (Byron and Brummell were frequent visitors) but lasted only twelve years. It closed in 1819 after its most frequent attenders ran out of funds.

Number 81 did not stay empty for long. Benjamin Crockford, who had started life as a fish merchant near Temple Bar, moved in to set up a gambling house for men of 'rank and breeding'. After a false start when loaded dice were found on the premises, Crockford put his house in order, insisting on propriety in all things while providing the finest food and wine at no cost to those who chanced their luck at the tables. It was a policy that paid handsomely, more than enough to build a luxurious gaming house at 50-53 St James's Street.

Intense socialising with copious eating and drinking gave eminent Georgians the bulbous paunches that the tightest corsets could not disguise. The benefit of exercise – a gentle stroll in the garden for ladies, horse riding and field sports for men – were offset by the overconsumption of fatty foods and heavy wines. Boisterous activity in the bedroom was thought to be therapeutic, 'I was afraid I was going to have gout the other day', wrote Lord

Carlisle to a friend. 'I believe I live too chaste; it is not a common fault with me.'

Standards of hygiene were not of the highest. The disposal of household waste was a community responsibility. In London it was financed by a 'scavenger tax'. Waste was collected two or three times a week and was taken to an official disposal site. But this did not include the removal of human excrement. This fell to private contractors who were also experts in recycling. Known as nightmen because they were only allowed to work between 11.0 pm and 5.0am, these enterprising entrepreneurs drove their carts to the nearest open country where night soil mixed with ashes was sold as a fertiliser. As London's outskirts expanded, finding sites for dumping waste became much harder, accelerating the sewage problem.

The image of London as a great sewer was adopted by Jonathan Swift for his poem *A Description of a City Shower*.

*Now from all the Parts the swelling Kennels flow,*

*And bear their Trophies with them as they go:*

*Filths of all Hues and Odours, seem to tell;*

*What Street they sail'd from, by their Sight and Smell.*

Water closets were an expensive custom built luxury and even the largest houses were limited to two or three conveniences, cleaned daily by servants. More modest homes had a privy, at best a simple shed over a bricked-in pit, often shared between several households. Chamber pots were kept under the bed. At formal dinners it was customary for a chamber pot to be kept in the sideboard for the convenience of guests after the ladies had withdrawn.

Yet men and women were fastidious dressers spending hours on perfecting their appearance. Even a man of moderate means such as James Boswell, Dr Johnson's biographer, had his hair powdered and dressed and his linen and underclothes changed every day. While full immersion in a bath was seldom practised, there was some justice in the common argument that wallowing in a tub of dirty water was hardly a guarantee of cleanliness. More in favour was a vigorous rub down with a wet flannel.

While heavily polluted water from the Thames was pumped up for everyday use (it was even argued by some that it had a curative value) fresh water was supplied by private enterprise. As early as 1609, Hugh Myddelton, a Welsh businessman, designed a forty-mile channel from the springs at Amwell in Hertfordshire to Islington in north London and thence to the City and the West End. Where the New River Company led the way, other suppliers of household water were soon available and underground sewers were built though haphazard disposal of waste with its attendant health risks was still prevalent.

Streets were poorly maintained. At night, torch-bearers were engaged to light the way round garbage tips and potholes. Other hazards included open coal-holes in the pavement for coal to be shot through to the cellars. Unwary pedestrians had been known to disappear into the void. Every smart house had its outside lamp which helped to light the streets though passers-by had to take care to dodge falling drops of oil.

The turning point in urban improvement was the Westminster Paving Act of 1762. For the first time, gutters were built at the roadside and in the main streets, Purbeck paving-stones replaced loose chippings. Pavements gave pedestrians protection against aggressive riders.

It was not only in Piccadilly that green spaces were disappearing under bricks and mortar. When the German linguist and writer J.H. Campe visited Britain in the 1790s he found London transformed from a medieval into something approaching a modern city.

> *The main streets are well paved, with excellent footways on*
> *either side on which four to six people could walk and pass.*
> *Oxford Street has a footway eight to ten feet wide, and a*
> *roadway in which seven or eight vehicles can pass with ease.*

Campe was amazed to count fifty-two coaches at one time in Piccadilly including what must have been a very early omnibus drawn by four horses with twelve passengers inside and sixteen on the roof, sitting on long benches face-to-face.

Horace Walpole complained of the crowds in Piccadilly who wandered into the road holding up his coach. At the same time, he was impressed by the rapid development of the neighbourhood.

> *I started to-day at Piccadilly, like a country squire. There*
> *are twenty new stone houses. At first I concluded that all*
> *the grooms that used to live there had got estates and built*
> *palaces.*

If the great houses of Piccadilly occupied a disproportionate amount of space for a privileged few, some account must be taken of the army of servants needed to maintain their lifestyle. An establishment the size of Devonshire House could boast a *maître d'hôtel*, a clerk of the stables and a clerk of the kitchen, a butler, cook, housekeeper, valet, gardeners, a coachman and his deputy, groom, footmen and footboys, chambermaids, housemaids, laundry maids, dairymaids and scullery maids.

Wages were modest but meals and lodging were provided. Moreover, the highest ranking servants could double their pay with tips and Christmas gifts from traders who were expected to pay for preferential treatment. A valued perk was the money that came from showing round visitors when the owners were safely out of town. Having the key to the wine cellar, the butler rarely paid for a drink.

Unquestioning obedience from servants was expected but rarely given. Dishonesty was compounded by ignorance and incompetence. An oft told story was of a housemaid who tore pages out of a book to light the fire. Since the volume had been left on a side table, she assumed no one had any further use for it.

The loose morality of Georgian England made Piccadilly open house for wealthy reprobates. Few left their mark except on IOUs. The exceptions are memorable for bringing a whole new meaning to debauchery. In a short life, the 7th Earl of Barrymore at 105 Piccadilly lived for excess as a gambler and womaniser. He excelled in the boxing ring and on the cricket pitch, and was one of the first of the aristocracy to act in public. He died aged 23 after accidentally shooting himself with his own musket. Left destitute by her husband's extravagances, his wife turned to prostitution. 105 was taken on by the sporting Isthmian Club before being rebuilt in the mid-nineteenth century on a grander scale than we see today.

One who lived life to the full yet managed to stay the course was William Douglas, 4th Duke of Queensbury, a world-class lecher. His critics said of him that he 'wallowed in sin'. For the second half of his life he lived at 138 Piccadilly at the corner turning into Park Lane. Designed to his specification, he moved into his new home in 1768. By then, Devonshire House had made the western end of Piccadilly highly fashionable. Aristocrats who had taken up residency included the Earl of Cholmondeley who built No. 139 while his brother, the General, occupied 137. Queensbury's less ostentatious house stood between the two.

Born in 1725, Old Q, as he became known in his maturity, was of Scottish descent, the only son of the Earl of March. After his father died young, the infant William was farmed out to his cousin, the 3rd Duke of Queensbury, whose country estate at Amesbury in Wiltshire, was not far from Stonehenge. The Duchess, Kitty, a warm-hearted mother of two sons, was only too happy to welcome William into the family circle, albeit surprised to encounter an aloof personality, apparently devoid of emotional depth. The countryside bored him though he did show an interest in horses. Grooms and stable lads taught him more than the books that were put before him.

William was at his best when the family decamped to their London base, Queensbury House, in Burlington Street, just off Piccadilly. It was here that William found that all things were possible or, at least, all the things that interested him such as sex, gambling and sex.

His chief weapon of seduction was charm. He was certainly not much to look at, with his large hook nose and small dark eyes. But society ladies were flattered by his talent for giving exclusive and devoted attention to whoever was in his sights. It helped that he was prepared to spend freely on what for him was a good cause.

As with seduction, so with gambling, his other great passion. Attention to detail was his abiding rule. He was prepared to take any bet as long as he could be certain that the odds were in his favour. A regular at Newmarket, he made a close study of form on and off the courses. A good judge of horse flesh he engaged the best jockeys to ride in his colours while he himself became a skilled rider. He was said to have won over a quarter million pounds on the turf.

Always ready to fleece the gullible he would open a book on seemingly impossible challenges which he would then overcome by unconventional means. So it was that he succeeded in sending a letter over fifty miles in less than an hour by wrapping it in a cricket ball to be thrown between twenty of the best in the game standing in a wide circle. His greatest coup was to design a lightweight horse-drawn conveyance that could travel at the then unheard of speed of nineteen miles an hour. A huge crowd gathered in Newmarket to witness William's triumph and to watch him claim his winnings.

William's Scottish inheritance on the death of his mother gave him wealth and social standing as Earl of Ruglen. But this was nothing compared to the great prize of becoming the Duke of

Queensbury. After the 3rd Duke's two sons died young, William found himself in the happy position of acquiring a prestigious title and enormous riches. He was now fifty-four but in good health and as promiscuous as ever. Despite the best efforts of eager matchmakers, he held off a chain of prospective brides. He was only too happy to welcome young ladies – the younger, the better – into his arms but his ardour cooled when it was suggested that he might formalise a relationship.

The nearest he came to a love match was an affair with a married dark-eyed Italian beauty. When Marchesa Fagnani became pregnant the blame was put squarely on William who accepted financial responsibility for his daughter while handing over parental duties to his only close friend, George Selwyn.

The two men had little in common. William was self-confident and shrewd, George, six years older, was gullible and indolent. Lord Carlisle described George Selwyn's life in town. 'You get up at nine; sit till twelve in your night-gown; creep down to White's and spend five hours at table; sleep till you can escape your supper reckoning and then make two wretches carry you in a chair, with three pints of claret in you, three miles for a shilling.'

George had no interest in women while William thought of little else. It was generally assumed that George was impotent. It he ever felt a sexual thrill it was when he indulged his fetish for attending public executions; the grizzlier the better. The paradox of an amiable loafer, fond of children and animals but with an 'attraction to the abnormal' was accepted by his friends with good grace.

'If Mr Selwyn calls,' said Lord Holland on his deathbed, 'show him up. If I am alive, I shall be glad to see him. If I am dead, he will be glad to see me.'

William was delighted that his friend was ready to take the role of surrogate father. For his part, George doted on the little girl he now decided to name Mie-Mie. Lavishing attention and responding to her every need, Mie-Mie grew up to be the archetypical spoilt brat; selfish and peevish when she could not get her way. As an adolescent she began to rival her father as a free-range lover. Five years before his death, William bought for Mie-Mie the house next door to 138 Piccadilly.

In his later years, Old Q was a star attraction of Piccadilly. A crowd would gather to watch him driving at speed in his dark green vis-à-vis carriage drawn by two long-tailed black horses with two servants behind him and his groom on horseback bringing up the rear.

He never lost his love of a wager. Notorious was his bet for a thousand guineas with Sir John Lode as to which of the two could put up a man to eat the most at one sitting. Old Q was not there to watch the match but he did have a witness on hand to report on the result. 'MY LORD, - I have not time to state particulars, but merely to acquaint your grace that your man beat his antagonist by a pig and an apple pie.'

Given his life of abandon, Old Q lived longer than anyone expected though he did have a full-time doctor on permanent duty, motivated by a generous fee to keep his patient alive. When his activity between the sheets was inevitably curtailed, he allowed his imagination free rein by setting up an observation post on his Piccadilly balcony. From here he could keep a beady eye on the ladies passing below. Shaded from the scene by a white awning, he ogled the pretty girls while he himself became something of a tourist attraction for giggling teenagers, one of the sights to be seen along with other less titillating ancient monuments.

Apart from maintaining a lively interest in sex, Old Q attributed his long life to a daily bath in fresh milk, a custom that prompted the well-founded rumour that having thoroughly cleansed the wizened body, the milk was recovered by his staff to be sold in the local market.

The Duke of Queensbury died, aged 85, in December 1810. Buried in a vault under the communion table at St James's Church, it was by his own request that no memorial tablet was erected. His Piccadilly house was split into two, one of which became home to Lord Byron for his brief married life.

Piccadilly's affluence attracted high class traders. At the corner where Bond Street connects to Piccadilly, on land once occupied by Clarendon House, Stewart and Watt Tea Rooms opened in 1688. The speciality of the house was the Piccadilly Cake, a popular delicacy heavy on cream and sugar. Stewarts continued in business until the 1950s when the building was reshaped for the London headquarters of Qantas.

Many other traders have come and gone. Richard Jackson, wax and tallow chandler occupied 190 Piccadilly while Thomas Hawkes, established in 1783, made military uniforms. Along Piccadilly and into Soho there were upholsterers, glovers, goldsmiths, tailors, milliners, jewellers, chemists, tea and coffee merchants, furriers, seedsmen and florists and scores of others.

Fortnum & Mason, purveyors of
fine provisions with a long
association with royalty

Of greater longevity and happily still with us is Fortnum &
Mason. When William Fortnum of Oxfordshire farming stock,
first came to London at the end of the seventeenth century, he
lodged with Hugh Mason who had a small grocery in St James's

Market adjacent to Piccadilly and the Haymarket. There was no immediate thought then of the partnership that would become world famous.

Luck was on the side of William when he landed a job as footman in the royal household. It soon occurred to him that he could supplement his wages by recycling discarded candle ends, rendering them down to make new candles. Having built up his savings, he decided to go into business on his own account. Since it was grocery that took his fancy it was only natural that he should turn to advice from his landlord and friend Hugh Mason. Together, in 1705, they set up a street stall not far from where now stands the modern Fortnum & Mason.

It was not a meteoric rise to prominence. While business expanded at a steady pace, it was not until the second half of the eighteenth century that it really took off. In 1761, Charles Fortnum, the 23-year-old grandson of the founder, followed precedent by entering royal service. From this vantage point he was able to make himself known to the assortment of officials with budgets for food, coal, house linen and wine. Charles was able to satisfy all their needs on advantageous terms for both sides. Retiring from palace duties in 1788 to give his full attention to a burgeoning business, he remained in place for eighteen years until selling his interest with 75 per cent going to his son Richard and 25 per cent to John Mason.

Meanwhile, Charles kept his influence at Court by becoming a Crown of the Chamber with access to all the people who mattered. The produce passing through the Fortnum & Mason warehouse became ever more exotic – poultry and game in aspic, 'decorated' lobsters and prawns, potted meats, hardboiled eggs in forcemeat (Scotch eggs), eggs soaked in brandy, topped by whipped cream, mince pies, savoury patties and fruits both fresh and dried 'all decorated and prepared so as to require no cutting'.

Officers with private incomes serving in the Napoleonic Wars insisted on their home comforts. 'I beg you to send me out hams, tongues, butter and cheese,' wrote one supplicant while another wanted a stock of candles, an order all too familiar in the early days of the firm.

*The Times* for December 30th, 1817, carried an advertisement for the latest Fortnum & Mason exotica.

*New Portugal Plums, Tours Plums, and French Dried*
*Pears, Fortnum & Mason take the earliest opportunity of*
*informing their friends that these fruits have been landed,*
*are in great perfection and may be had at their warehouse,*
*185 Piccadilly; the Portugals in the usual round boxes, and*
*the Tours Plums, dried apples and pears in small square*
*baskets, together with a very choice variety of Foreign*
*Fruits. Owing to the handsome packages, the above are*
*particularly adapted for Presents.*

After the accession of Queen Victoria, the sale of tinned food was extended to ready-roasted duck with green peas, a whole truffled pheasant and West Indian turtle. Such delicacies served at top class dinners attracted royal patronage across Europe. At home, Fortnum & Mason became Foreign Warehousemen to H.R.H. the Prince of Wales (Edward VII) and Purveyors of Oilery to H.M.The Queen (Victoria).

Annual events in the social calendar such as Derby Day and the Harrow and Eton cricket match at Lords, caused traffic jams in Piccadilly as coaches and carriages jostled for parking to collect hampers, the queue beginning to form at first light. 'If I had a horse to enter for the Derby,' wrote Charles Dickens, 'I would call it Fortnum & Mason, convinced that with that name he would beat the field.'

In June 1886, a young American turned up at 181 Piccadilly with five sample cases of canned goods. His sales pitch was a triumphant success. Fortnum & Mason took the lot. Nine years later Mr Heinz opened his own London branch to sell the famous 57 varieties.

Rebuilt in the mid-1920s to give more display space to attract the passing trade, in 1951 the company was sold to Canadian business mogul, Garfield Weston who embarked on another period of expansion. The clock with its revolving figures was placed prominently on the façade in 1964 as a tribute to the founders of Fortnum & Mason.

Bookselling and publishing were second nature to Piccadilly. With money and leisure, residents provided a ready market. One who spotted a business opportunity was John Hatchard. His diary entry for June 30th, 1797 reads:

> *This day, by the grace of God, the good will of my friends and £1 in my pocket, I have opened my bookshop in Piccadilly.*

He was not without experience. Having served his apprenticeship with a Westminster bookseller, at age twenty-one he had joined a rival establishment in Castle Street where now stands the National Gallery. Though the shop was small it served as a meeting place for the intellectual elite. Hatchard worked hard on his contacts who were soon to provide him with a loyal customer base in Piccadilly.

With his evangelical background, he was a natural ally of anti-slavery campaigner William Wilberforce, the guiding spirit of the Clapham Sect, 'a network of friends and relatives ... bound together by their shared mood and spiritual values'. Dedicated to good works and noble causes they organised petitions and public meetings, lobbied politicians and published a journal, *The Christian Observer*. Hatchard was at the centre of this frenetic activity.

Soon after opening his shop, he published a best-selling pamphlet, *Reform or Ruin; Take Your Choice*. The author was John Bowdler, father of the better known Thomas Bowdler who achieved notoriety with his expurgated versions of Shakespeare's plays.

Propelled by his early success, Hatchard was made publisher of *The Christian Observer* and of the *Reports of the Society for the Bettering the Conditions of the Poor*, of which Wilberforce was a founder member. It was at Hatchards that Wilberforce built up support for the abolition of slavery. He even had an office on the premises; Hatchard was delighted to be of service. The club-like environment he fostered was good for business. Those who talked books, bought books.

Writing in the *Edinburgh Review*, Sydney Smith poked gentle fun at Piccadilly's literary coterie. 'This is a set of well-dressed prosperous gentlemen who assemble daily at Mr Hatchard's shop; clean, civil personages well in with the people in power ... and every now and then one of these personages writes a little book and the rest praise that little book, expecting to be praised in their turn for their own little books.' John Hatchard presiding in his black frock coat and waistcoat buttoned to the throat, could have been mistaken for a superior *maître d*.

Hatchards, one of the oldest established
bookshops noted for its Royal Warrants

Such was John's success, after four years he felt able to move
to larger premises at 189-190 (now 187) Piccadilly. And that is
where Hatchards has remained.

With the spread of literacy in the early nineteenth century,
the book trade prospered. Overall, by the 1820s, some fifteen
thousand were employed throughout the country on printing,
binding and the sale of books, two thousand of them in London
alone. With its famous address, Hatchards became a popular
meeting place for societies with only a marginal connection to literature; The Royal Horticultural Society, for example and, more
oddly, the Outinion Society set up to advise and supply helpful
information to those who wished to marry.

After John's retirement, aged 80, the family connection was maintained by his son Thomas who died in 1858. The business then passed to Henry Hudson, John's great grandson. By then Hatchards had foregone publishing to concentrate exclusively on book selling. That it continued to prosper was in large part thanks to A.L. Humphreys who joined as a junior assistant in 1881. It was Humphreys who established a reputation for putting together libraries for stately homes. Whether the books were ever read is another matter.

Hatchards is now part of the Waterstones chain of bookshops. The Waterstones flagship store at the Circus end of Piccadilly overshadows Hatchards physically but in no way detracts from the appeal of the smaller shop which retains the bibliophilic feel of earlier times.

Waterstone's flagship bookshop, one of the finest inter-war buildings, was created for Simpsons, a leading men's outfitters

# 4

# Literary Lives

As booksellers made their mark in Piccadilly, publishers were quick to follow. When, in 1812, John Murray moved his premises from Fleet Street to 50 Albemarle Street, he had already made a name for himself as the publisher of the Tory leaning *Quarterly Review*, a literary and political periodical that set itself against the Whiggish *Edinburgh Review*.

Murray's appearance on the Piccadilly literary scene was not welcomed by rivals such as James Ridgway who, operating from 170 Piccadilly, had a nice thing going publishing polemical essays. But this was to assume a static market. The truth was otherwise. With the expansion of literacy there was a growing demand for entertaining and instructive literature. John Murray had an eye for talent backed by an instinct for sound business.

With an author list headed by Jane Austen, Lord Byron and Walter Scott, he was soon at the head of his profession. Washington Irving dubbed him 'the prince of booksellers' though

Jane Austen was more grudging; 'He is a rogue, of course, but a civilised rogue.'

John Murray, publishers of Lord Byron, Jane Austen
and many other top ranking authors, was based just off
Piccadilly at 50 Albemarle Street

With John Murray playing the ever genial host, Number 50 became a salon for writers and their admirers, all of distinction if not always literary. Murray was a sympathetic listener to the troubles of the cultural elite. 'The hours of access are from two to five,' wrote Washington Irving. 'It is understood to be a matter of privilege, and that you must have a general invitation from Murray.'

Murray's attempts to balance his commercial interests against his innate desire to be accepted by the social elite, was to cause him multiple problems. Meanwhile, everyone wanted to be published by Murray. Declared Samuel Smiles, author of *Self-Help* which sold 20,000 copies in its first year, Murray 'was inundated with poems and novels from all parts of the country'.

A shrewd decision was to add Jane Austen to the Murray list. The opportunity came about as Jane's brother Henry, a none-too-successful banker and army agent had an office in the courtyard at Albany. With good looks and irrepressible charm, Henry was a social asset but an unreliable partner in any money-making enterprise. Blind to his defects but counting on his commercial experience, it was only natural for Jane to turn to her favourite brother to help find her a publisher for *Northanger Abbey*, the first of her completed novels.

It is likely that Jane visited Henry when she was in town though the related correspondence was destroyed after her death. In any event, the manuscript of *Northanger Abbey* was handed over to Henry who sold it outright, as was then the custom, to Crosby and Co. of Ludgate Street. Jane received £10, by no means a princely sum at a time when a middle class family needed up to a thousand a year to live in comfort. The contract having been signed unconditionally, there was no pressure to fix a date for publication. Messrs Crosby sat on the manuscript for six years.

Her patience exhausted, Jane decided to test the waters by writing to her publisher in waiting. Using an assumed name, she chided Richard Crosby, albeit gently, for his dilatory style of business. 'Tho' an early publication was stipulated at the time of sale, I can only account for [the delay] by supposing the MS by some carelessness to have been lost.' She offered a replacement copy adding, 'should no notice be taken of this address, I shall feel myself at liberty to secure the publication of my work, by applying elsewhere.'

She received a dusty answer. Crosby denied emphatically that he was under any obligation to publish. Moreover, if any other publisher tried to muscle in he would take action to prevent the sale of the book. But he did offer to return the manuscript to the author at the price paid for it.

Unfortunately for Jane, after the death of her father in 1805, the family could ill afford to recover her property. *Northanger Abbey*, not her best book but better by far than most first novels, was left to Richard Crosby for a further four years while Jane found other subjects to write about.

*Sense and Sensibility* was published in 1811 by Egerton's of Whitehall who made a bad job of the printing. However, two editions sold well enough to give Jane a modest profit. She stayed with Egerton for *Pride and Prejudice* and *Mansfield Park* with mixed results which decided her to offer her next novel, *Emma*, to John Murray. The manuscript was handed over to William Gifford, editor of the *Quarterly Review* and Murray's assessor of new work. He was impressed, having 'nothing but good to say'.

With Henry leading the negotiations, Murray made an offer sufficient to prise Jane away from Egerton while leaving the publisher with the lion's share of any profits. Thus emboldened, Henry, no longer a banker but now a Church of England clergyman, was able to buy back the copyright for *Northanger Abbey*. It gave him pleasure to tell Crosby that the author of the book he had surrendered, known to him only by a pseudonym, was also the author of *Sense and Sensibility*, *Pride and Prejudice*, *Mansfield Park* and *Emma*. Jane did not live long enough to see *Northanger Abbey* in print. It was Henry, the ever-loving brother who navigated the novel through its final stages to publication in 1818. Murray subsequently published *Northanger Abbey* and *Persuasion* in a single volume. But there was still a long way to go before Jane Austen became a national treasure, the darling of literary studies.

If recognition for Jane Austen was slow to evolve, fame came easily if fleetingly to Matthew Gregory Lewis, a resident of Albany, whose softcore porn novel *The Monk* was an immediate bestseller. Though there were strict laws against obscene publications, an exception was made where the frank portrayal of sex could be interpreted as a warning of the awful fate in store for transgressors. This was how Lewis got away with his seminal novel. Published in 1795, when Lewis was just short of his twentieth birthday, *The Monk* follows the misadventures of Antonia, an innocent virgin, but not for long, who falls victim to Ambrosio, a lecherous mendicant. In describing their encounter, Lewis does not hold back.

*He clasped her to his bosom almost lifeless with terror, and faint with struggling. He stifled her cries with kisses, treated her with the rudeness of an unprincipled barbarian, proceeded from freedom to freedom and, in the violence of his lustful delirium, wounded and bruised her tender limbs. Heedless of her tears, cries and entreaties, he gradually made himself master of her person, and desisted not from his prey, till he had accomplished his crime and the dishonour of Antonia.*

Scarcely less vivid is the earlier seduction of Ambrosio himself, debauched in his monastery by the fiendish Matilde who threatens:

*'Either your hand guides me to paradise, or my own dooms me to perdition' … As she uttered these last words, she lifted her arm, and made a motion as if to stab herself. The friar's eyes followed with dread the course of the dagger. She had torn open her habit, and her bosom was half exposed. The weapon's point rested upon her left breast: and oh! that was such a breast! The moon-beams darting full upon it enabled the monk to observe its dazzling whiteness: his eye dwelt with insatiable avidity upon the beauteous orb: a sensation, till then unknown, filled his heart with a mixture of anxiety and delight; a raging fire shot through every limb; the blood boiled in his veins, and a thousand wild wishes bewildered his imagination.*

To keep up the momentum, Lewis adapted his formula of sex with violence to the stage. But this time he overdid it. The impact of *The Captive*, a melodrama about a woman chained in a dungeon, was so realistic that audiences shrieked with terror and women went into hysterics. The play was taken off.

For the rest of his short life, Mat Lewis, or Monk Lewis as he was soon known to the world at large, enjoyed an active social round, his notoriety compensating for his limitations as a dinner companion. Of small stature ('the least man I ever saw', said Walter Scott) with bulging eyes, he was a great talker, rarely giving anyone a chance to get a word in. As a friend and admirer, Byron called him 'a jewel of a man' while adding 'If he would but talk half and reduce his visits to an hour, he would add to his popularity.'

Albany suited Lewis perfectly. His taste in furnishing was idiosyncratic.

> *He had 'almost a passion for mirrors' and his rooms were*
> *full of them, with flowers and books and pictures and*
> *here and there 'little elegant devices and poetic fancies'.*
> *He was constantly adding to his collection of bijouterie*
> *and 'all sorts of pretty knick-nackery', particularly of seals*
> *for which he was 'continually inventing new mottoes and*
> *devices'. His friends were sure of pleasing him if they gave*
> *him another seal.*

Lewis was emotional and easily moved to tears, a tendency that made him an object of fun. When the Duchess of York bestowed generous praise for his work, his eyes welled up. 'Never mind,' said a friend. 'I'm sure she didn't mean it.'

Lewis inherited from Byron a faithful if unconventional servant, a huge bearded Venetian, Giovanni Battista Falcieri, known as Tita. Outliving his master by more than a half century, this temperamental giant (Byron recorded that he had stabbed two or three people) ended his days as a messenger at the India Office.

Apart from his writing, Lewis had another source of income that was even more controversial, based as it was on plantations in the West Indies where more than five hundred slaves laboured on behalf of the family fortune. While the slave trade had been abolished, those already in captivity had no hope of early liberty. Treated as cheap labour they were forced to work to the point of collapse in order to keep down the price of sugar, a much sought after luxury.

Lewis was not without conscience. On dining terms with William Wilberforce and other prime movers for the abolition of slavery, he accepted that slavery was an evil. But he and many chose to believe that freedom would result in 'a general massacre of the whites'.

Lewis decided to find out for himself how conditions on his plantations could be eased. At the end of 1815 he set sail from Gravesend. His *Journal of a West Indian Proprietor*, published in 1834 by John Murray, records his first impressions of Jamaica.

> ... *the dark purple mountains, the shores covered in mangroves of the liveliest green down to the very edge of the water, and the light-coloured houses with their lattices and piazzas completely embowered in trees, altogether made the scenery of the Bay wear a very picturesque appearance.*

Getting down to business, an inspection of his estates revealed barbaric practices.

> *I am indeed assured by everyone about me, that to manage a West Indian estate without the occasional use of the cart-whip, however rarely, is impossible; and they insist upon it, that it is absurd in me to call my slaves ill-treated, because,*

> *when they act grossly wrong, they are treated like English*
> *soldiers and sailors. All this may be very true; but there is*
> *something to me so shocking in the idea of this execrable*
> *cart-whip, that I have positively forbidden the use of it on*
> *Cornwall [his estate]; and if the estate must go to rack and*
> *ruin without its use, to rack and ruin the estate must go.*

In demanding changes that made standards bearable for his work-force, Lewis held to the popular conviction that the natives were incapable of running their own lives. In his journal for January 5th, 1816, he wrote:

> *While Mr Wilberforce is lamenting their hard fate in*
> *being subject to a master, their greatest fear is not having a*
> *master whom they know, and that to be told by the negroes*
> *of another estate that 'they belong to no master' is one of the*
> *most contemptuous reproaches that can be cast upon them.*

He was back in Jamaica by the end of 1817 to find that his attempt to ameliorate conditions on his plantation had fallen short. Identifying eight supervisors who were worse than 'petty tyrants', he sacked the lot, calming his maltreated workforce while still finding time to add to his collection of negro songs and stories. Whether Lewis's good intentions bore fruit is open to question. He himself did not live long enough to find out. On the way home from his second venture to the West Indies, he caught yellow fever. He died at sea in May 1818, aged 43.

A journal entry for March 28th, 1814 records Lord Byron's introduction to Piccadilly life.

*This night got into my new apartments [in Albany], rented of Lord Althorp, on a lease of seven years. Spacious, and room for my books and sabres.*

Confident of his talent and eager to make his way in the world, Byron was a young man in a hurry. There were, however, formidable obstacles. He had a title but no money. The family seat, Newstead Abbey, was in such poor shape it was impossible to live there. While making the most of his youthful good looks, he was inclined to stoutness which he combatted with strenuous exercise. A deformity in one foot made him morbidly sensitive to a limp he did his best to disguise. Capricious and wilful, he had great charm that dazzled, if only briefly. He could quickly become morose.

Having wandered Europe from 1809 to 1811, Byron returned to London with the first two Cantos of *Childe Harold's Pilgrimage*, a semi-autobiographical narrative poem about a young man's pursuit of absolution for a life of idleness and debauchery.

The rights were taken up by John Murray but not without reservations. Leaning towards Toryism, he was nervous of Byron's more acerbic observation on the political scene. When the poet refused to tone down his views to please the 'Orthodox', Murray decided nonetheless to press ahead with publication. The first edition of *Childe Harold* appeared in March 1812 and after a slow start achieved, said Murray, 'unprecedented sales', 4,500 copies in less than six months, a bestseller by the standards of the day. Byron shot to fame, the idol of London society.

A succession of women fell to his embrace. He treated them all abominably. Then, having moved into Albany, Byron embarked on a widely publicised affair with Lady Caroline Lamb, wife of William Lamb, Lord Melbourne and future prime minister who had spent his early years in what had been Melbourne House, then York House and latterly Albany.

The quiet, bookish Melbourne had been under no illusions when he married Caroline. At seventeen, she was intelligent and vivacious with a wild streak that was liable to surface without warning. Her background did her no favours. Her mother, Harriet, Countess of Bessborough, was the sister of Georgiana, Duchess of Devonshire and a distant cousin of Charles James Fox. What Caroline learned of life came from the Piccadilly social set. It did not encourage discipline or restraint.

When, in 1803, Caroline had reached the age of 18 and was preparing to enter the adult world, she was already acquainted with her future husband. After their first meeting he resolved that 'of all the Devonshire House girls, she is the one for me'. Caroline was equally besotted. Though shy and withdrawn, he was kind and attentive. Even so, it was not until his brother's death in 1805 when he became heir to his father, Viscount Melbourne, that Caroline accepted his proposal. Now styled Lord Melbourne, he was married to Caroline on June 3rd, 1805.

As a forewarning of what was to come, on her wedding day, Caroline had a fit of hysterics. William must have reckoned that marriage would contain her passionate nature. If so, he was wrong. Rather, her capriciousness and self-indulgence became all the more apparent. The consequences of her unpredictable temper were invariably blamed on William for failing to keep her under control. For his part, he infuriated Caroline with his refusal to be provoked. By 1810, they had settled on independent lives while still sharing a home.

On the hunt for a personality mercurial enough to match her own, Caroline fastened on to Byron. The favourite guest of every London hostess, the literary lion was easy to meet. But the first encounter fell short of her expectations.

> *There limped into the room a self-conscious youth, with a handsome sulky head, fidgety movements, showy, ill-fitting clothes and a manner conspicuously lacking in the ease and naturalness usual in a man of his rank. Indeed, Byron at twenty-four was, in almost every respect, the opposite of the version of himself he sought to impose on the world.*

Nonetheless, Caroline was mesmerised by one who could match her ebullient and contradictory nature. Byron was 'bad, mad and dangerous to know' she decided, which was as good as saying that she found him irresistible.

Their tumultuous affair was a fight to the finish, both set on making an impression on the world which took no account of sensibilities, their own or those of anyone else. Byron was the first to declare the game over. Longing to be quit of a relationship that threatened his sanity, he found a sympathetic counsellor in Caroline's mother-in-law. At sixty-two, Lady Melbourne was flattered by the attention of society's most sought after young man and was only too happy to advise on seeing off 'the little beast', as she was known by the family.

Byron's move to Albany was an attempt to shut himself away from his troublesome lover. He might have known he could not succeed. While given to hysterical fits, Caroline was well up to adopting male disguise to gain entry to his chambers. Two months after taking up residence, Byron was complaining to Lady Melbourne of 'an inroad which occurred when I was fortunately out' and a month later, 'You talked to me about keeping her out. It is impossible; she comes at all times, at any time, and the moment the door is open in she walks.' When Lady Melbourne urged extra security, Byron assured her that 'all bolts, bars, and silence can do to keep her away are done daily and hourly'. It was not enough.

Returning one day to his apartment, he found on the title page of a book he had left open the words 'Remember me'. In response he wrote:

*Remember thee! Remember thee!*
*Till Lethe quench life's burning stream*
*Remorse and shame shall cling to thee,*
*And haunt thee like a feverish dream!*

*Remember thee! Aye, doubt it not,*
*Thy husband too shall think of thee:*
*By neither shalt thou be forgot,*
*Thou false to him, thou fiend to me!*

Cruel, but not without justice.

Though he hardly acknowledged it, Byron had reason to feel gratitude to the aggrieved husband who looked on his wife's lover as a fellow victim. When Caroline was at Brocket Hall, he did his best to calm her and could not bear to see her humiliated.

*One day she was making arrangements for a dinner-party at Brocket. Exasperated at what she considered the stupidity of the butler in failing to grasp her ideas of decoration, she suddenly leapt on to the dinner table, and fixed herself in a fantastic attitude which she requested him to take as the model from which to arrange the centrepiece. The poor man, terrified by her extraordinary appearance, ran to William for help. He came immediately. 'Caroline, Caroline,' he said in tranquillising tones, and gently lifting her from the table carried her from the room.*

Byron found a line of escape into marriage to Lady Melbourne's niece, Annabella Milbanke. The marital home was 13 Piccadilly Terrace. It proved to be a false move. Annabella was highly intelligent but held to a strict code of conduct that did not at all suit wayward Byron. His loutish behaviour which included telling his wife that he had married her only to be revenged on her for turning him down two years earlier, poisoned the relationship. A deed of separation was signed on April 21st, 1816. Byron departed England settling for a time in Geneva before resuming his travels and his numerous love affairs, eventually taking up the cause of Greek independence from Turkish rule. He died of a fever in 1824. Caroline outlived him by four years. Too unbalanced to manage life on her own, she lived at Brocket while William kept to his official home in London, returning occasionally to see how she was getting on. Badly was the answer.

The long drawn-out struggle destroyed Caroline's vitality. Spending her days in the monotony of rural seclusion, she descended into premature senility, sustained by alcohol and laudanum. Her dependence on William was complete, and she knew it. He was, she confessed, 'the only person who never failed me'. William was by her side when she died, aged forty-two on January 25th 1828.

Byron's death left John Murray with an agonising problem. Inevitably, as paymaster and friend of the wayward poet, Murray could not ignore the affair with Caroline Lamb. Though he tried to keep his distance he was dragged into the combat when Caroline turned up at Albemarle Street with a letter, purporting to be from Byron, requesting that a miniature portrait of himself be handed over. Murray agreed reluctantly only to find that the letter was a forgery. A stern rebuke was treated by Caroline as a joke. She signed her response, 'Horatio Nelson and Lady Hamilton'.

Murray's frustration was mollified by Byron's continuing success. After the publication of more of *Childe Harold* came the first two cantos of *Don Juan*, a work that thrived on the hostile criticism of conservative journals. Blackwood's described it as 'a filthy and impious poem'. Murray pressed on with the publication of the remaining cantos while feeling the strain of attack by his Tory friends. But the cash machine could not be switched off. Murray offered Byron 2,000 guineas (over a million pounds today) for his memoirs.

While work was cut short by Byron's early death, Murray was left to decide whether or not to publish what was already extant. He turned to William Gifford whose advice was unequivocal. The memoirs, he said were 'fit only for a brothel and would doom Lord Byron to everlasting infamy if published'. As editor in waiting, Thomas Moore accepted the need for cuts but came up against the uncompromising view of Byron's close friend John Hobhouse who argued for the destruction of the manuscript. Murray agreed. So it was that the last work of one of the great poets was consigned to the flames in the fireplace of 50 Albemarle Street. It was not John Murray's finest hour.

Of all the troubled souls who sought refuge in Albany, Edward Bulwer-Lytton was among those for whom the urge to self-destruction was strongest. Judged in his day to be a great novelist, he outsold Dickens and Thackeray. But his 'silver fork' stories exposing the cruel duplicity of high life have not worn well. Remembered now chiefly for the opening line of his novel, *Paul Clifford*, 'It was a dark and stormy night', his chief failing was his verbosity. That famous opener would have been more effective had it not been followed by lengthy and tedious scene setting.

Lytton's personal troubles started with his marriage. At age 23, he fell in love with Rosina Wheeler. Similar backgrounds brought the young couple together and similar backgrounds drove them apart.

Heir to the ancestral home at Knebworth, Lytton had had little to do with his bully of a father. Instead, he had clung to his adoring autocratic mother. Of melancholic imagination, inclined to self-pity, he lived for the books handed down by a scholarly grandfather.

Rosina suffered equally from paternal neglect. To compensate for a drunken waster of a father, she had a strong willed mother ambitious for her daughter. The beautiful Rosina was a romantic who yearned to be the inspiration and life force for a high-flying artist.

No ordinary housewife she. For his part, Lytton wanted a clever wife who would serve him as a docile helpmate. The two roles were incompatible. Rosina allowed herself to be swept along on a soppy fantasy that she and Lytton were tragic orphans cast into a hostile world. 'We are alone ... let us cling to one another for support.'

Lytton's mother opposed the match, seeing Rosina as a destroyer who would cut off her son's talent before it had a chance to bloom. Caught between two determined women, Lytton indulged in fits of self-pity. After the couple married in August 1827, his mother refused to acknowledge her daughter-in-law and stopped Lytton's allowance forcing her son to make what he could from writing until he came into his inheritance.

In perpetual fear of debt, Lytton worked on reviews, essays and books to support lavish expenditure. Literary success came with *Falkland* (1827), *Pelham* (1828) and *Eugene Aram* (1832). His workload did not help the marriage. A shared pleasure in childish pursuits such as having visiting cards printed for their favourite dogs was no deterrent to fierce rows and an almost sadistic pleasure in giving emotional hurt. Two children were born; Emily in June 1828 and Robert in November 1831, both to be victims of family discord. By 1834, the marriage was over.

Escaping to Albany in 1835, Lytton sought comfort with less demanding female admirers. Beside herself with jealousy, Rosina set out to prove that the security of Albany was not all it was cracked up to be. Late one night, she gate-crashed Lytton's chambers where she claimed to find evidence of his infidelity, specifically two teacups on a table, a shawl draped over a sofa and the figure of a woman disappearing into her husband's bedroom.

Descending to hysteria, Rosina made a half-hearted attempt at suicide, stabbing herself with a dinner knife. In 1838, her children were removed from her care on grounds of neglect.

Lytton had his supporters, notably Charles Dickens who told his friend that Rosina 'is the misfortune of your life'. She was certainly a pain, not least for Dickens who incurred her wrath for joining Lytton in a fund-raising evening of amateur theatricals to raise money for writers who had fallen on hard times. Specially written for the occasion, Lytton's five act comedy, *Not As Bad As We Seem*, required a setting sufficiently resplendent to attract those with deep pockets. The choice fell on Devonshire House. When he gave his consent, it is unlikely that the Duke realised what he was in for. As rumours circulated of Rosina's intention of disrupting the performance, elaborate efforts were made to keep her at a safe distance. The concern was all the greater for the announcement that Queen Victoria and Prince Albert were to be guests of honour. Rosina wrote to the Duke warning him that she would appear disguised as an orange-seller with the weapons to hand to pelt the Queen, if not with oranges, then with rotten eggs.

With guards on all entrances and uniformed heavies patrolling Piccadilly, any lady who resembled Rosina, even remotely, was subject to intrusive scrutiny. In the event, the errant wife stayed away, doubtless satisfied at having caused the performers, including Dickens himself, a severe attack of stage fright. Circulating a parody of Lytton's play called *Even Worse Than We Seem*, Lytton was made to look ridiculous.

With Rosina winging off letters to Lytton's clubs and to his friends, he resorted to force. Abducted on the street, Rosina was packed off to a private asylum. She was released a month later, the result of a press campaign led by *The Telegraph*.

Inevitably, it was the children who suffered. The 19-year-old Emily died alone in a lodging house in the Brompton Road. When Rosina attempted to see her she was forbidden entry by a doctor acting on Lytton's instructions. His claim to have rushed to his daughter's side and that she had died in his arms was pure fantasy.

Lytton cut a pathetic figure in his declining years. A drift into sentimental medievalism was accompanied by a fascination with the occult and spiritualism. His last books were pessimistic projections into the future when socialism had swept away the old values. His eccentricities were notorious. In his house in Charles Street he had a room fitted as an exact replica of one in Pompeii.

Lytton died, aged 70 in 1873. Rosina followed in 1882.

# 5
# Wonder World

Opposite the Burlington Arcade and hard by the Piccadilly Arcade, passing notice might be made of Egyptian House, a block of offices at numbers 170 to 173. Why Egyptian? Something to do with cotton, perhaps? In fact, the name is all that remains of the once famous Egyptian Hall destined to be one of London's most popular venues catering for the Victorian passion for combining entertainment with self-improvement.

The Egyptian Hall was hard to miss. Inspired by Nelson's victory at the Battle of the Nile, it had a yellowish façade embellished with hieroglyphics. Two gigantic Egyptian deities, Isis and Osiris, with distinctive headdresses and ornate kilts, stood above the entrance bearing on their heads a large canopy. Beneath their feet, cut in stone, was the single word 'EXHIBITION'. On each side were red brick houses with small balconies where the occupants must have wondered what they had done to deserve such an unconventional and incongruous neighbour.

The Egyptian Hall, a venue for the weird and wonderful

The outward appearance of the Egyptian Hall had little connection with what went on inside. It was commissioned by William Bullock who wanted, and got, an eye-catching exterior to attract paying customers to see his collection of fifteen thousand 'natural and foreign curiosities'. Those included, among the Napoleonic relics, the Emperor's bullet-proof coach complete with kitchen and dressing room captured at Waterloo.

After Bullock sold out in 1825, the Egyptian Hall with its interior based on the Temple of Karnak near Luxor, was adapted to live entertainments. Freak shows were among the biggest draws. There were queues to see David Lambert, the fat man of Leicestershire who, at age about thirty, weighed eighty-seven stone.

Yet more sensational was General Tom Thumb. His real name was Charles Stratton and he came from Bridgeport, Connecticut.

The rise to fame of this teenage midget, twenty-six inches high and less than twenty pounds in weight, was masterminded by the legendary American showman, Phineas T. Barnum, who taught his protégé how to sing and dance and encouraged his skill as a mimic.

An American tour was followed by engagements across Europe. By now Tom Thumb was an international celebrity. After appearing at the Egyptian Hall, Barnum worked his social connections to secure an invitation for the General to entertain the Queen at Buckingham Palace. Tom Thumb was the talk of the town and the money rolled in.

The public fascination with a performing midget did not extend to an exhibition in one of the adjoining galleries. It was here that Benjamin Haydon set out to demonstrate art as a 'delightful mode of moral elevation' with huge canvasses illustrating *The Burning of Rome*, *Daniel in the Lion's Den* and *Noah's Ark*. Haydon was mortified by seeing the crowds pass by his gallery intent on seeing General Tom Thumb. 'Tom Thumb had 12,000 people last week', he wrote. 'B R Haydon, 133½ (the ½ was a little girl)'. Overcome with frustration, the impecunious artist cut his throat.

The phenomenon of Tom Thumb set the bar for other performers who hoped to fill the Egyptian Hall. The one who came closest was the ebullient Albert Smith whose speciality was the illustrated travelogue. He had built his reputation on a stage show called *The Overland Mail*, recounting his adventures on the new route between Britain and India across the Egyptian desert. Audiences who rarely ventured more than a few miles from home were enthralled.

Smith performed in front of a moving canvas, twenty-feet high and several hundred feet long, wound round a spool hidden behind the proscenium. His talk was interspersed with songs and what one reviewer called 'histrionic representations of fellow travellers'. Critics were impressed with his talent for making 'prepared material seem spontaneous and intimate'.

Casting about for another crowd-pulling spectacle, Smith turned to the Victorian obsession with the mystery, romance and danger of mountain peaks. As the highest summit in the Alps, Mont Blanc had first been climbed in 1786, but since then few had attempted the challenge and even fewer had succeeded. *Murray's Handbook for Travellers* warned against risking lives, adding that many of those embarking on the ascent 'have been persons of an unsound mind'.

The first British climber (though Canadian-born) to make the ascent was a 22-year-old geologist, John Auldjo, in 1827. His account of the achievement caught Smith's imagination. Though short, stout and middle-aged and thirteen years older than Auldjo, Smith set about hiring guides for an assault on the mountain.

Smith may have embroidered some of the perils he encountered but who could doubt the terror of using a ladder as an improvised bridge over a crevasse? 'With a chasm of unknown depth below,' he wrote, 'it is satisfactory to get to the other side as quickly as possible.'

Nearing his objective, Smith suffered such severe altitude sickness that he hallucinated and collapsed. But he staggered (by some accounts he was carried) to the top, where he 'fell down upon the snow and was asleep in an instant'.

Back in London, Smith set about turning his adventures into a stage performance. The Egyptian Hall was given an Alpine makeover complete with a two-storey Swiss chalet, jagged rocks and a running stream.

While Smith interspersed his lecture with songs and jokey representations of those he met on his perilous route, panoramic scenes of Mont Blanc unfolded vertically. In the interval, St Bernard dogs carried boxes of chocolates for the youngest members of the audience. An industry of tie-in products ranged from board games to hats and fans. A Mont Blanc quadrille was a favourite in ball rooms and dance halls.

The Ascent of Mont Blanc ran for seven seasons to July 1858. It was around this time that the Egyptian Hall began to face serious competition. In 1843, the government finally got over its fears of the theatre as a subversive influence. No longer was the Lord Chamberlain able to withhold on any grounds a licence for presenting plays; his role now was to act only 'in the interests of good manners, decorum or the public peace'. The result was a boom in theatre building.

The Egyptian Hall found respite by reinventing itself as 'England's Home of Mystery', appealing to families with young children. The inspiration came from two highly inventive magicians, Maskelyne and Cooke, who were able to persuade audiences to doubt their senses. To create an atmosphere where magic could be expected, the interior was made dark and spooky. Yet no possible offence could be taken at anything that happened on stage. While there were thrills galore, parents and their offspring felt safe in the Egyptian Hall.

*The most amazing things happened. A man named David Devant did wonderful conjuring and kept so many plates on the spin altogether at the same time that the senses reeled with them. He never let one fall down. There was a remarkable organ; there was a kind of trick orchestra which really was a forerunner of that marvel of the films, stereophonic sound, for it played 'The Death of Nelson' from all sorts of unlikely places in the building and filled its listeners with wonder. That organ, too, pealed out 'The Bay of Biscay' with terrific effects in the way of thunder and lightning, more than a little frightening to nervous children who got some strange thrill out of it all the same.*

The 'trick orchestra' mentioned came about after Maskelyne was visited by a Lincolnshire farmer who announced that he had invented a mechanical man capable of arithmetic, spelling and smoking. Ever willing to try something new, Maskelyne made the journey to Lincolnshire to see for himself this amazing 'automaton'. It was everything he had hoped for. In partnership with its creator, Maskelyne suggested a few modifications to what became the famous Psycho. Later joined by Zoe, they soon took second place to a mechanical cornet player called Fanfare. At his first concert in April 1878, Fanfare played 'I know a bank where the wild thyme grows' and joined in the duet 'Hearts and Homes' with his owner. After Labial, a euphonium player made his appearance, Maskelyne played trios with the two automatons taking a third part on cornet or tenor horn. His technique was said to be inferior to that of the fabricated musicians. 'Fanfare and Labial,' wrote Maskelyne's son Jasper, 'were scholarly little men with the long locks and dreamy eyes of true musicians. One sat on a chair, the other on a music stool. They performed sweetly and accurately any popular piece of music asked for by the audience. No works were apparent, no clockwork ticking or whirring was audible, there were no electric wires or airpipe connections. There they sat, mysterious, complacent, and earnest, and a good deal more human than some modern musicians I have met.'

So impressed was A.J. Phasey, euphonium player to Queen Victoria, he wrote to *Musical World* to express his fears that 'at some future time, living performers in orchestras may be replaced in favour of automatons'.

Jasper, Maskeylne's son, described one of his father's most popular illusions:

*He appeared on stage carrying what looked like a bundle of arms, legs and general human assortments. These he dumped on the floor, picking them up one by one and exhibiting them to show that each was genuinely separate.*

*Then he would take the trunk, clap a leg on to it – and, hey presto, the leg stuck! Then would come an arm, clad of course in the sleeve of a jacket, since each portion of anatomy was already dressed in the appropriate portion of garment. The arm was pushed against the trunk, and stayed in its place.*

*Another leg followed; then the second arm. The head, its eyes open and intelligent and its hair glossy and curling, was raised and stuck on to the neck of the trunk.*

*At this point my father waved his wand – and the figure began to speak in a human voice, to laugh, to slap its creator on the back; and finally, after adjust his tie, it walked solemnly off stage. It was obviously real.*

When the Magic Circle, a club for illusionists was founded in 1905, Maskelyne was its first chairman.

Maskelyne and Cooke were quick to exploit moving pictures. An 'Animated Photograph' of Queen Victoria's funeral had attracted interest but this was as nothing compared to the speeding train, seemingly roaring out of the screen, straight at the audience.

After thirty-one years at Egyptian Hall, a.k.a. the House of Mystery was a mystery no more. It fell to the wrecking ball in 1905.

# 6

# An Ever Changing Scene

Early in the nineteenth century, the pre-eminence of Piccadilly came under threat from a formidable rival, a new boulevard from Regent's Park, itself created from pasture land, to what was soon to be Piccadilly Circus and on to St James's.

If Regent Street was the vision of the Prince of Wales, later George IV, it was made real by the architectural genius and shrewd businessman John Nash who gave practical shape to the 'greatest shopping mile in the world'.

Nash was fifty-seven when he entered upon the most creative period of his life. By his own account, this 'thick, squat dwarf figure with a round head, snub nose and little eyes' was not obviously destined for greatness. His early years as a builder-architect led him to bankruptcy but he managed to keep himself afloat on commissions from country house owners. His fortunes changed for the better when, at age forty-six, he married an ambitious young woman who had ingratiated herself into royal society. There were rumours, strong though never confirmed, of an affair with the Prince of Wales. True or not, Nash acquired money and influence.

From 1811, the Prince and Nash were actively plotting Regent Street as a 'Royal mile', an elegant boulevard with luxury shops and exclusive apartments acting as a divider between the aristocratic West End and the crowded, chaotic Soho where six to a room was the common lot of families on the margin.

With work held up by the Napoleonic War, it was five years before Regent Street progressed beyond the drawing board. The plan to forge a straight line between two fixed points had to be amended to accommodate disobliging landlords. The solution, though costly, proved to be the outstanding distinction of Regent Street, a gentle curve towards the Circus which Nash called the Quadrant.

Nash gave himself heart and soul to the project. Not content with acting as chief architect, he raised capital from the Royal Exchange Assurance Company and the Bank of England while promoting the sale of leases and even speculating, not always successfully, on his own account. His chief ambition, to make Regent Street a centre for 'taste and fashion' was quickly realised. Max Beerbohm spoke for many when he described Regent Street as 'a happy hunting ground for ardent shoppers'. The down side was pressure from the shopkeepers to have things their own way at the expense of the architectural vision. The prime example was the opposition to the lining of the Quadrant with a colonnade supported by 270 cast iron columns. The idea was to provide a covered promenade for pedestrians, protecting them from rain and wind. The shopkeepers failed to get the point. For them, it felt as if they were being cut off from the passing trade. They also feared that the colonnade would harbour unsavoury characters who might deter legitimate customers.

With Regent Street all but completed, the authorities were eventually persuaded that the ironwork had to go. Sold by auction, the columns were snapped up by railway companies to add lustre to new stations but twenty of them remained in London and are still to be seen at Drury Lane Theatre where they line the stage-door side of the building. For many years they provided a covered way for playgoers queuing for the cheaper seats.

Nash went on to lay out the Mall, and Carlton House Terrace, rebuilt Buckingham House to create Buckingham Palace and transformed a bare, marsh tract into St James's Park.

As the nineteenth century progressed, Piccadilly lost its reputation as a secluded enclave. Those rich enough to live well back from the road could lead peaceful lives but for middle class residents in and around Piccadilly the district became noisier and at the same time, more colourful, not least after dark with the adoption of gas lighting making it easier and safer to move about the streets.

Horses hooves clip-clopping over cobbles set up a constant din, starting early in the morning with dustcarts, followed by deliveries of milk, meat, vegetables and general provisions each with their own conveyance. To this cacophony was added the cries of the vendors competing in volume to alert householders of their presence. On frequent visits would come the apple-woman, bellows-menders, flower-sellers and knife grinders, all shouting their services. Until late in the century, women in shawls and bonnets carried a yoke on their shoulders bearing pails of fresh milk.

Over fifty butchers in Piccadilly and Mayfair drove in live-stock from outlying farms for slaughter next to their shops. Many of the larger houses had their own cowsheds as well as fully staffed stables. With coachmen, stable boys, harness cleaners and grooms, the mews to the rear of the mansions, which today are garages or flat conversions, were a world apart.

Piccadilly was a starting point for the mail coaches making for Bath and Bristol. 'The finest sight in the metropolis is the setting off of the mail coaches from Piccadilly,' said William Hazlitt.

*The horses paw the ground and are impatient to be gone, as if conscious of the precious burden they convey. There is a peculiar secrecy and dispatch, significant and full of meaning, in all the proceedings concerning them.*

*Even the outside passengers have a correct and supercilious air, as if proof against the accidents of the journey; in fact, it seems indifferent whether they are to encounter the summer's heat or the winter's cold, since they are borne through the air on a winged chariot. The mail carts drive up and the transfer of packages is made, and at a given signal off they start, bearing the irrevocable scrolls that give wings to thought, and that bind or sever hearts for ever. How we hate the Putney and Brentford stages that draw up when they are gone! Some persons think the sublimest object of nature is a ship launched on the bosom of the ocean: but give me for my private satisfaction the mail coaches that*

*pour down Piccadilly of an evening, tear up the pavement,*
*and devour the way before them to the Land's End.*

On the corner of Dover Street was the Old White Horse Cellar, a famous coaching inn. It was one of seven taverns serving passengers waiting to board the coaches. The others were the White Bear, the Gloucester Coffee House, the Hatchett's Hotel, Webb's Hotel and, one of the oldest, the Hercules Pillars. The galleried yard of the Three Kings at 75 Piccadilly survived into the twentieth century.

A frequent visitor to the Pillars of Hercules was the Marquis of Granby whose name was to be adopted by so many public houses. Commander-in-Chief of the British army from 1766, Granby was noted for his concern for the welfare of his men. When a retired soldier set up as a publican, a common change of career, it was only natural for him to name his pub after his old commander.

Victorian morality was a late developer. As the symbol of all that was bashful and straight-laced, Queen Victoria was more than thirty years into her reign before the loose living of Georgian culture was finally contained. Writing of *London in the Sixties*, Captain Donald Shaw (his real identity is uncertain) tells us that the whole area south of Piccadilly was thick with night houses. A few steps from Piccadilly Circus, Panton Street was said to be 'the very sink of iniquity and abominations of every kind'.

If Shaw's melodramatic style invites scepticism, greater reliance can be put on the recollections of Fyodor Dostoevsky who visited London in 1862. Of the Haymarket he wrote:

*It is the district where in certain streets at night the prostitutes gather in their thousands. The street is festooned with gas jets in a way of which at home we have no conception. At every step there are superb cafés all gilt and glass. You meet your friends there – and you take refuge there. It is painful to mix with the crowd. Its composition is so strange. You find there old women and beauties at whom you gaze, dazzled. Nowhere in the world is a type of woman as beautiful as the English. The dense crowd moves with difficulty. The pavement does not suffice for it and they invade the road. They are all thirsty for prey and recruit the firstcomer with complete cynicism. Grand clothes rub shoulders with rags; the same contrast in age; everything is mixed up. You hear curses, quarrels, shouts, and the engaging whisper of a lovely girl who has not yet lost her shyness ... In the Haymarket I have seen mothers putting their little daughters up for sale. Children of twelve seize your arm and want to follow you.*

Trafficking in children continued unabated until exposed by the journalist W.T. Stead who proved to a doubting world that it went on when he bought a girl of thirteen from her mother, took her to a bawdy house, then had himself arrested.

Dance halls were a perfect cover for illicit activities. The Argyll Rooms, offering gambling and dancing, at the Circus end of Piccadilly, was a gathering place for high-class prostitutes 'magnificently dressed in silks, satins and seal-skins'. An entrance fee of one shilling with another shilling added on to gain admission to the lavishly-furnished galleries ensured that only the well-off gained entry.

In winter, prostitutes who fell short of the standards of the exclusive preserve but counted themselves a cut above the normal run, gathered in the Burlington Arcade (the 'temple of frippery and frivolity') where, for a consideration, the beadles turned a blind eye. Rooms above the Arcade shops were rented out for dubious purposes while on open sale were the dyed green carnations, the badge of availability for gay sex. Even so, there were basic rules of convention to be observed. A fragrant abuse of what was regarded as minimum decency was liable to attract the attention of the police. In 1871, Ernest Boulton and Frederick Park, cross-dressers, otherwise known as Fanny and Stella, were hauled up before the magistrate for 'conspiring and inciting persons to commit an unnatural offense'. A Burlington Arcade beadle was among those who confirmed the couple's lifestyle.

The Argyll Rooms, along with numerous brothels, were closed down in 1878. But prostitution continued to thrive, a reminder for today that Victorian rectitude, so often thought to be ubiquitous, made marginal impact on London's West End. It was said of any scarcity that it was as rare as a virgin in Piccadilly.

Respectable residents of Piccadilly voiced their protest. When the street walkers intruded on the forecourt of Albany, Thomas Mortimer, a solicitor, proposed putting up gates at the Vigo Street entrance, 'to shut out disorderly persons', only to be brushed off by the Secretary who pointed out that the narrowness of the entrance 'would render gates inconvenient' and that 'if erected, they would require an additional porter, bringing upon the trust considerable expense'.

Mortimer was not so easily put off. In 1814, he wrote angrily to the Secretary:

> *It seldom happens that I return to my chambers in the evening that I am not obliged to pass the entrance to get rid of unfortunate females rather than allow them to follow me to my door, even after I have submitted to the contributions which the lower orders invariably beg, and a close pursuit has compelled me sometimes to knock at the front door of the Great House rather than my own in order to deceive them as to my residence.*

Acknowledging the complaint but still reluctant to spend money, the Trustees tried to push the responsibility on to the public authority. That didn't get far though it was agreed to move the Watch Box from the bottom of Sackville Street to 'a situation as near as possible to the entrance of the Court Yard of Albany'.

Prostitution was too much part of the social scene to be tackled by piecemeal measures. The typical streetwalker would get up in the afternoon, walk the streets for an hour or two and, if her luck was in, take a client home. If business was short, she would make for the Haymarket or Hell's Corner, as it was known, 'haunted by rouged and whitewashed creatures, with painted lips and eyebrows and false hair', according to the medical writer, Dr William Acton.

Of all the night haunts in Haymarket, unrivalled for notoriety was Baron's Oyster Rooms which was in such a state of dilapidation that beams had to be knocked into place to hold it together. Until luck ran out.

*Ominous cracks and groans warned the revellers that all was not right, [Then] ... a sound that vibrated like the crack of doom caused a stampede, and leaving wine, oysters, hats, unpaid bills, every one rushed helter-skelter into the street. Old Baron, staring disconsolately from the pavement at his fast-collapsing house, suddenly appeared to remember that his cash-box was in the doomed building, and rushing frantically in, was seen hurrying out with his prized treasure. And then a crash that might have quailed the stoutest heart rang through the night, and Barron, cash-box, and lights, all disappeared in a cloud of dust that ascended up to heaven. Days after the old man was found firmly clutching his treasure.*

Moralists suffered agonies of despair at the base instinct of the male species. In railing against those who were no higher than the beasts of the field, Francis Newman, brother of Cardinal Newman, blamed the 'School Classics' which 'perniciously inflame passions in boys and young men', a surprising view from one who had been professor of Latin at University College, London for seventeen years.

There were eating places that catered almost exclusively for riotous evenings. St James's Restaurant, now the site of the

Piccadilly or, latterly, the Dilly, Hotel, was known to every young blade out for a good time as Jimmy's. It was not a place where he would take his bride but he might take someone else's wife.

> *Many wild pranks were played at 'Jimmy's', and pandemonium often reigned supreme when bright sparks, having turned the gas off at the main, proceeded to toss a couple of hundred hats to all quarters of the room. It takes little imagination to realize the number of free fights that occurred when the lights went up again and rightful owners struggled to regain their property. Many were the battles fought in a blackout at 'Jimmy's', oyster shells and plates being the favourite ammunition. On these occasions shelter under the tables was the safest place, even after the barrage had died down, for more often than not fisticuffs were indulged in between the originators of the mêlée and those injured in the fracas. Any damage caused was always well paid for, and it was on very rare occasions that the police were called in to restore order; and when they did appear, friend and foe turned on the intruders, resenting being interfered with by strangers in uniform.*

Young bucks on a spree were liable to get out of hand. At the Pic, where hat smashing was the thing, the destruction of a tall hat invited a bare-knuckle fight. A dinner in celebration of Shakespeare's tercentenary in 1864 descended into chaos.

> *... and serious trouble started when some scene-shifters with voracious appetites began sending their plates up for*

*more and more ham and the wags who were serving piled*
*them indiscriminately with meat, custards, oranges, and*
*marmalade. ... Soon dishes and plates were flying in all*
*directions. Even the waiters joined in.*

At Kate Hamilton's, the underground night house between Piccadilly Circus and Leicester Square, where the big money congregated, young men underwent their rite of passage. Kate Hamilton was a monstrous figure of unashamed debauchery.

'She weighed at least twenty stone,' wrote Bracebridge Hemyng, 'and had as hideous a physiognomy, with a bodice cut very low, this freak of nature sipped champagne steadily from midnight until daylight and shook like a blancmange every time she laughed.'

Open spaces were a draw for unsavoury characters, particularly after dark. The reputation of Green Park suffered accordingly. Along the Piccadilly side of the Park was a wall 'against which ballads were sold by day and robberies committed by night'. In November 1862, the *Saturday Review* reported that 'Piccadilly after midnight is nearly as unsafe as Hounslow Heath a hundred years ago'.

But on summer evenings it was quite different. It was then that Green Park hosted a parade of celebrity and fashion, the *haut ton*, when full evening dress was *de rigueur* for a stroll on the Queen's Walk. This ran by the side of a reservoir supplying fresh water for the royal households of Westminster. It was a romantic spot though also known for the suicides it attracted.

Such was the appeal of the *haut ton* for spectators that it gave added value to the houses at the back of Arlington Street with windows overlooking the park. As the century progressed, Green

Park lost out to St James's Park, becoming 'for the most part, a bare plot of ground, little used except by those who cross it to go to Westminster from the West End'.

Attempts to improve the image included replacing the wall between the park and Piccadilly by railings with flower beds along the entire length. But it was St James's Park that had the edge.

'It is the smallest of all the parks,' wrote Max Schlesinger, 'But it is a perfect jewel amidst the splendid buildings which surround it on all sides. On its glassy lake fine shrubs, and beeches, and ash-trees on the banks throw their trembling shadows; tame water-fowl of every description swim on it or waddle on the green sward near, and eat the crumbs which the children have brought for them. The paths are skirted with flower-beds, with luxurious grass-plots behind them; and on sunny day these grass-plots are crowded with happy children, who prefer this park to all others, for the water-birds are such grateful guests, and look so amiable and stupid, and are so fond of biscuits, and never bite anyone. And the sheep, too, are altogether different from all other sheep in the world; they are so tame and fat, and never think of running away when a good child pats their backs, and gives them some bread to eat. And there are green boats, and for one penny they take you over to the other side; and the water, too, is green, much greener than the boat; and there is no danger of horses and carriages, and children may run and jump about without let or hindrance, and there are such numbers of children too. In short, there is no saying how much pleasure the London children take in St James's Park.' Despite its drawbacks, Piccadilly remained the first choice of residence for those who could afford it. In 1838, Lionel de Rothschild took up occupation at number 148, between Hamilton Place and Hyde Park Corner, part of an eighteenth century terrace that was gradually transformed into a set of palatial mansions. Rothschild House was expanded over the years to create a conservatory, a grand staircase, basement offices under the garden and, after merging with number 147 in the 1850s, a vast new hallway and reception rooms.

The style, said the architectural critic and cartoonist Osbert Lancaster, combined all the richest elements of those which had preceded it. 'The heavy golden cornices, the damask hung walls, the fringed and tasselled curtains of Genoese velvet, the marble and parquet' were reminiscent of the wealthiest circles of Venice. The excess of gilt was not to everyone's taste but as Lancaster commented, 'it was a style that at least possessed the courage of its opulent convictions'.

The Rothschild family was the darling of Piccadilly bus drivers not because a Rothschild ever travelled on a bus but because on one day a year every driver and conductor was gifted a brace of pheasants. By way of thanks, drivers tied to their whips a bunch of ribbons of yellow and blue, the Rothschild colours.

# 7
# Two Exceptional Women

Number 23 Piccadilly was the setting for a scandalous *ménage à trois*. It was here that the renowned beauty Emma Hamilton shared her favours with her husband Sir William Hamilton and her lover, Britain's foremost naval commander, Admiral Horatio Nelson.

Emma's rise from poverty to the giddy heights was a story of what could be achieved, even in a rigidly defined society, by a woman of brains and determination. Born in 1765 into the harsh confines of a mining community, the daughter of a blacksmith who died young, Emma was raised by a devoted mother and grandmother. At age twelve she made her way to London to earn a living as a housemaid. But not for long. Having failed to break into acting she found employment as a barmaid and tavern waitress with an occasional lapse into prostitution, where her teenage allure attracted wealthy clients. And not just those in pursuit of sex. The more glamorous brothels such as Madame Kelly's on Arlington Street off Piccadilly, were visited by artists in search of the ideal model – compliant and affordable. Emma became a favourite of Joshua Reynolds and of the portrait artist, George Romney whose paintings of her in classical poses were to secure her a lasting fame.

Emma Hamilton, celebrated mistress
of Horatio, Lord Nelson

Pregnancy interrupted Emma's advancement. In need of a protector she fastened on to the 32-year-old Charles Greville, second son of the Earl of Warwick, a collector of antiquities, keen gardener and half-hearted politician who installed her in a small house on Paddington Green, then a rural suburb. Greville was a bore who gave Emma scant respect or affection. His chief aim in life was to find an heiress desperate enough to marry him. Happy to take a cut of Emma's earnings as an artist's model, he nonetheless baulked at the expense of maintaining a mistress and resented her popularity with people of influence.

Eager to be free of mother and child, Greville hatched a plot to foist Emma on his uncle, Sir William Hamilton, Envoy Extraordinary to the Kingdom of Naples. Unaware that the arrangement was intended to be permanent, Emma set off on her latest adventure in March 1786, just short of her twenty-first birthday.

Emma's reception in Naples was better than she might have expected. While happy to avail himself of her services, Hamilton was kind-hearted and considerate. His passion was for Roman and Greek culture and for building his collection of ancient vases. He looked upon Emma as some sort of erotic decoration, a living throwback to the classical ideal. For her part, Emma made no attempt to usurp Hamilton's fragile wife. But she was ever eager to put on a show. Visiting dignitaries were bowled over by an enchantress who could sing, dance and, in a loose fitting costume, perform a succession of classical and erotic poses. It was not long before Emma had made herself indispensable. With the death of Hamilton's wife, it seemed only natural that he should offer to formalise the relationship.

Emma knew her own best interests. As Lady Hamilton she was free to move in Neapolitan court circles where she became a close confidante of Queen Carolina. This was at a time when there was fear of an overspill from the French Revolution. Carolina's sister Marie Antoinette had died on the guillotine. Emma brought comfort by promoting an English alliance but the arrogant and duplicitous King Ferdinand put his faith in French good intentions, unaware that Napoleon already had plans to invade Naples.

He reckoned without Britain's Mediterranean fleet under the command of Horatio Nelson.

A decisive sea battle was fought at Aboukir Bay at the mouth of the Nile. A more conventional commander might have held back from taking on thirteen French ships of the Line including the enormous *L'Orient* with 120 guns and a thousand men on board. Nelson however, was not in the least conventional. The attack started at 5.30 in the afternoon. The cannons roared throughout the evening until at 10 o'clock *L'Orient* blew up. The explosion was heard for miles around. As the great ship sank it took with it over half a million pounds in bullion along with treasures Bonaparte had looted from Malta.

Savouring his triumph, Nelson made for Naples for recuperation and the refitting of his ships. Emma put herself at the head of the welcoming party. Nelson must have been startled at the effusive greeting from a 31-year-old beauty whose openly declared devotion knew no bounds. Caught in a loveless marriage, Nelson was only too happy to be swept off his feet. What Emma hoped to gain is harder to determine. While military prowess can be a powerful aphrodisiac, Nelson was short on physical appeal. A small man, thin and pale with an unruly shock of red hair, he was missing his right arm and was badly scarred over one blind eye. But that Emma was smitten there could be no doubt. It was not long before the gossip was of a raging affair. The visibly ailing Hamilton looked on with a benign eye, content that his Emma had found happiness.

However, life was not trouble free. Nelson's presence in Naples made a French invasion inevitable. With King Ferdinand of Naples a born loser and the acme of incompetence, the decision was taken to evacuate the royal court and its camp followers. Nelson, now rear admiral and with a knighthood, put himself in charge of an operation that, technically, was Hamilton's responsibility.

Returning to London, Nelson was welcomed at 23 Piccadilly, where the Hamiltons had recently taken possession. By now an affair between Nelson and Emma was common knowledge. Hamilton gave silent consent, refusing to take umbrage even when Emma gave birth to a girl who had unquestionably been sired by Nelson. If there was any doubt, naming the baby Horatia gave the game away.

Encouraged by Nelson, Emma spent freely while her husband petitioned in vain for government compensation for the losses he had suffered in Naples. Hamilton died in 1803, Emma holding him in her arms with Nelson at his side.

Banking on the wealth that would come their way after Nelson had fulfilled the promise of more victories at sea, Emma made scant effort to economise. But having gained little from Hamilton's legacy, she did move to a smaller house in Clarges Street while Nelson took up lodgings in nearby Dover Street.

Nelson's affair with Emma did not go down well at Court where Queen Charlotte made it clear that Emma would not be made welcome. Even Nelson himself had a frosty reception, the King commentating disparagingly on the array of medals, several of foreign origin, which Nelson flaunted. His reception was 'not very flattering' recorded a friend. 'His Majesty merely asked him if he had recovered his health' before turning away to talk to an obscure general.

Over the next two years which saw the death in infancy of a second child, the lovers kept up a stream of correspondence which ended with Nelson's death at Trafalgar. A devastated Emma was left with a pile of debts. As the creditors moved in and with the government keen to be rid of an embarrassing encumbrance to the memory of Britain's saviour, she and her daughter decamped to Calais where they lived, if not quite in poverty, certainly in straightened circumstances.

The 'divine lady' as she was called by George Romney, the painter for whom she had sat no less than twenty-four times, died in January 1815. She was nearly fifty.

꧁꧂

On the corner where Stratton Street meets Piccadilly lived Angela Burdett-Coutts, one of Europe's richest women. As the grand-daughter of Thomas Coutts, the sole proprietor of Coutts Bank (we met him earlier as the financial backer of Albany) Angela Burdett-Coutts, as she became known, hoped to live comfortably. But in her younger days she had no expectation of acquiring great wealth.

For one thing, her immediate family did not fit well into a social circle that put great store by financial and political stability. Her father, Sir Francis Burdett, having married into the Coutts family, proved to be an unreliable husband and, more controversially, a political maverick. After election to the House of Commons, he campaigned energetically for the abolition of corporal punishment in the army and spoke out for universal male suffrage. Denied the sympathy of his wife Sophia, he found comfort in the arms of Lady Oxford who was 'warm, vital and uninhibited'.

Burdett landed himself in serious trouble with an open letter to his constituents denying the right of the Commons to imprison anyone who offended its exaggerated sense of privilege. The result was a Commons vote to punish Sir Francis for his 'libellous and scandalous paper' by sending him to cool his heels in the Tower of London. Burdett's many supporters were not having that. A crowd gathered at his Piccadilly house on the corner of Bolton Street to stop the warrant being served. Sir Francis held out for three days, the doors bolted and barred, while the mob howled its anger against the persecutors. It was only when the military was called to restore order that the beleaguered politician allowed himself to be handed over to what were dubbed the 'Piccadilly Butchers'. He was held in the Tower for only a short time. Having made its point, the Commons ordered his release. Thereafter, Sir Francis settled for a quieter life, at home and in politics. Angela was the child of a reconciliation between Francis and Sophia.

What Thomas Coutts thought of all this can only be imagined. But while the banker conveyed to his ever expanding roster of aristocratic clients an image of sober gravity, he was by no means cast in the conventional mould. Instead of marrying into the clan that provided him with his substantial income, he had chosen as his wife the daughter of a Lancashire farmer who had worked for his brother as a housemaid. She had presented him with three daughters. However, Coutts was not the stay-at-home type. In his later years, his wandering eye fastened on to an actress famed more for her beauty than for stage talents. Her name was Harriot Mellon.

The child of a broken marriage, Harriot started her career as a strolling player, visiting booths and barns in Lancashire and Yorkshire. Spotted by Richard Brinsley Sheridan, she joined the cast of his comedy *The Rivals* at Drury Lane to play uncredited bit parts. Advancing to leading roles, she attracted a bevy of wealthy admirers. At their head was Thomas Coutts. While their relationship was close, Coutts had no intention of breaking up the family home. It was not until his wife died in 1814 that he made a formal proposal. He was then eighty. The couple had seven contented years before Harriot came into an inheritance of close on a million pounds and a house looking out on Piccadilly from Stratton Street.

Though middle aged, she was still turning heads, her appeal now enhanced by her income. Of the many offers of marriage, there was only one she took seriously, that of William Aubrey de Vere, 9th Duke of St Albans. It was said, cynically, to be an ideal match; Harriot liked the idea of being a duchess while her suitor was in urgent need of funds. The chief gift to the gossip mongers, however, was the difference in ages. Harriot was twice as old as her husband. Yet by all accounts, it was a happy marriage. It ended after ten years with Harriot's death. Remarkably, given the dominant male role sanctified by law, Harriot had secured a marriage settlement that had left her in sole control of her fortune which had continued to grow.

Even more remarkably, after a generous allowance for the Duke, she left everything to the youngest of the granddaughters of Thomas Coutts. Angela Burdett was now very rich indeed. A deeply religious, socially withdrawn young lady, Angela was bewildered by the unexpected turn in her affairs. Her two sisters, who had never got on with Harriot, were furious at being cut out from their step-grandmother's largesse. Angela did her best to restore peace with generous endowments.

She had a harder time fending off her suitors. For years she was stalked by a wild-eyed deranged and impecunious lawyer who refused to accept that he was not the love of her life. Doubtless it was to deter unwanted attention that Angela who, by the terms of the Duchess's will had changed her surname to Burdett-Coutts, made no attempt to look attractive. A spinsterish appearance gave her an air of severity that was not in her character.

While the Duke of St Albans was permitted to remain in the town house for the rest of his life, Angela's tour of the premises she was eventually to occupy, did nothing to diminish her wonderment of her turn of fortune. 1 Stratton Street was a treasure house, magnificently furnished in Harriot's dramatic style.

*The bow windows of the downstairs drawing-room were curtained with gold damask, the walls lined with blue, fluted silk. There was a superb India-Japanned screen, display tables with yet more scent bottles; up the scarlet carpeted stairs, the great drawing-room was even more splendid. The chairs were black and gold, there were swagged golden curtains, rich cut-glass chandeliers and, reflected in the mirrors, and dominating the room, Chantrey's huge marble statue of Thomas Coutts. In the library on the second floor, was an astonishing range of books, reflecting Thomas Coutts's wide-ranging taste.*

Gradually adapting to her new life, Angela had to think what to do with her money. To leave it sitting in the bank was not an option. With Christian charity as her guiding principle, she was soon in pursuit of noble causes to benefit the poor and oppressed.

Her status as a woman of independent means, the granddaughter of one of the foremost bankers of his day, gave Angela an entry to the corridors of power. Latching on to Charles Dickens who lamented the thousands of children in London who were 'hunted, flogged, imprisoned and not taught' she worked with him to set up 'ragged schools' to provide basic learning. In 1846, she enlisted Dickens's support in setting up a charity to help former prostitutes make a fresh start in the colonies.

Angela admired strong personalities. Though he was out of sympathy with much of her do-gooding, the Duke of Wellington was a close admirer though not so close as to accept a marriage proposal. He excused himself on grounds of age. Social housing was one of Angela's many philanthropic causes though her good intentions were not always appreciated. In London's East End, the purpose built Columbia Market, a Gothic pile designed to meet the highest standards of hygiene, was rejected by local street traders who feared over-attentive health officials.

Moving into Stratton Street in 1837, Angela gained confidence in her public role. Though she was never 'the great lady', her banquets were lavish with the table set with Sèvres china and gold plate. Her balls were less successful. It was said that too many bishops in attendance dulled the proceedings. Her greatest personal extravagance was collecting china, pictures and rare manuscripts.

Philanthropy was her first love. In addition to model housing at affordable rents, she built two churches and endowed church schools. A friend of Florence Nightingale, she paid for a drying machine to be sent to the Crimea so that soldiers would not have to wear wet clothes. A co-founder of the London Society for the Protection of Cruelty to Children, she was also, more improbably, the first patron, later President, of the British Goat Society. The owner of several goats, she was convinced of the healthy properties of goat's milk.

In 1871 she was created Baroness Burdett-Coutts. It was an honour she was not sure she deserved. Of more value to her was the title bestowed on her by the East End, the Queen of the Poor. A familiar sight in Piccadilly where she often sat at her bow window to take in the view, she was gratified by the cheers of the crowd.

In the autumn of her life, Angela sprang a surprise on her friends and admirers by following the example of her step-mother in marrying a man half her age. Her choice fell on an obscure young American, William Ashmead Bartlett. After the forthcoming marriage was announced in July 1880, Angela came under intense pressure to change her mind. She was not dissuaded, and rightly so, for Bartlett proved to be a devoted husband. They remained happily together for twenty-five years until Angela's death at the age of 92 in 1906. After a lying-in-state at Stratton Street, this remarkable woman was buried in Westminster Abbey at the foot of the memorial to Lord Shaftesbury, her friend and fellow benefactor of the poor. Her house on Piccadilly was demolished in 1925.

# 8
# Dining In and Dining Out

That peculiarly British institution, the gentleman's club, began to make its mark in the mid-eighteenth century when popular coffee and chocolate houses converted to members only, attracting those of shared background or occupations. But any resemblance to the modern club was purely incidental.

The history of White's in St James's Street, a few steps from Piccadilly, bears witness to changing times. Now the most exclusive of all London clubs, White's has its origin as a chocolate house in Chesterfield Street managed by Francesco Bianco who anglicised his name to White. In 1778 he relocated to St James's

Street to establish a club catering, chiefly, for rich, idiosyncratic Old Etonians. It focussed on election of candidates who were devoted to gambling for high stakes.

An identifying feature of White's was its bow window where celebrity members condescended to passers-by. The elegantly-tailored dandy, Beau Brummell, self-appointed arbiter of male fashion, who introduced full-length trousers to succeed knee breeches and stockings, invariably claimed central place though not always to the liking of those of higher breeding. 'Damn the fellow,' bellowed a peppery colonel. 'He's an upstart, fit only for the society of tailors.' Brummell did not stay the course. Ruined by gambling he departed to France to die in poverty. Posterity has been kinder with a recently erected statue in Jermyn Street.

The three oldest surviving London clubs are White's and its near neighbours, Boodle's and Brooks's. Originally divided along political and social lines, the Tory patrician belonged to White's, the Whig politician of old family gravitated to Brooks's while the gentlemen up from the country favoured Boodle's.

Along with a bevy of rules to what members could or could not do, odd conventions were rigidly adhered to. In one club change was given in washed silver. The money was dipped into hot water before being put in a porous bag. This was whirled round in the air until the coins were dry. At White's, a mahogany dining table had a net built in at the centre where corks were collected. It was the only sure way of calculating how much wine had been drunk.

The Victorian age introduced formality. The new clubs that sprang up on Pall Mall were solidly built for solid citizens. The first to open its doors was the United Service Club (now the Institute of Directors) on the corner of Waterloo Place. Three years later, in 1830, the Athenaeum opened on the opposite corner. The first catered for senior officers, the second for 'men of science, literature and art'. A sign of the times was the well-stocked library created at the Athenaeum. An earlier generation would have dismissed such an amenity as a waste of space. Thackeray was among those who made good use of the library, spending so much time there he had a desk reserved for him.

Next door to the Athenaeum, the Travellers Club, 'founded to encourage the exchange of ideas between Englishmen and foreigners', invited candidates who had ventured five hundred miles from home. But a long-distance journey was not of itself a sufficient qualification for election. In 1895, Cecil Rhodes was shocked to hear that he had been blackballed. On his rise to fortune, he had made too many enemies.

Further along Pall Mall, the Reform was for supporters of the 1832 Reform Bill which abolished corrupt boroughs and extended the franchise to the middle class. Nearby, the Carlton was favoured by those of the opposite persuasion. It moved to 69 St James's Street after German bombs destroyed the original building. The University Club, demolished in 1906, was at the corner of Pall Mall and Suffolk Place while the Union Club, now Canada House, occupied the north side of Trafalgar Square.

The Reform was one of the first clubs to offer overnight accommodation. It was also noted for the high standard of its kitchen, presided over by Alexis Soyer, one of the great chefs. On the other side of Pall Mall, the Army and Navy Club had no such distinction. So bad was the food, the voluble Captain

William 'Billy' Higginson Duff, said to be 'a colourful character with an undistinguished military career', dismissed it as a 'rag and famish affair', a reference to a disreputable gaming house. In response, members who were more easily satisfied, adopted the Rag and Famish, later shortened to The Rag as the club byname. The Oxford and Cambridge opened in St James's Square in 1830, moved to its new premises in Pall Mall seven years later.

Piccadilly had its own parade of clubs, nearly all within shouting distance of each other. At number 94, the Naval and Military occupied the former home of the Earls of Egremont and subsequently of Lord Palmerston, when it was called Cambridge House. Known as the In and Out by the two signs set in stone on the outer wall to ease the flow of coaches, the club moved to St James's Square in 1999. At the time of writing, the original premises are being converted into a luxury hotel.

Of the clubs that have long since closed their doors, St James's, favoured by diplomats, occupied 106 Piccadilly, one of the finest eighteenth century houses, while next door was a sporting club called the Isthmian (a nod to the games of ancient Greece) on the site of the one-time Pulteney Hotel. With more than the usual number of young members, the Isthmian was known as the Crèche. Lady guests were welcome but they had their own entrance, a custom soon adopted by other clubs to show they were not entirely misogynistic.

At No. 95 was the American Club; at 96, the Junior Naval and Military; at 100, the Badminton; at 101, the Junior Constitutional; at 116, the Junior Athenaeum; at 119, the Cavendish and at 138, the Lyceum, all now part of history.

No. 107 became the Savile Club until, in 1927, it moved to larger premises in Brook Street. Also of longer duration (it is still there today) is the Cavalry Club which moved into No. 127 in 1890, before doubling its size nearly twenty years later. A close neighbour but of more recent vintage is the Royal Air Force Club.

Just off Piccadilly, in Hamilton Place, the Bachelors Club was founded in 1881 to become the favourite of society hostesses looking to fill their invitation lists for their daughters' coming out balls. The Club eased the way by circulating the private addresses of its members. Somehow, wrote Ralph Nevill, 'it escaped even the faintest breath of censure'.

More contentiously, the Albemarle Club, founded in 1874, was open to both sexes. After a slow start, it was doing well by the 1880s when it suffered from the fallout from the Oscar Wilde trials. Bizarrely, the feminine influence on club life was associated with decadence. The club moved to Dover Street in 1909 and eventually merged with the In and Out where the progressive view of women's rights was not a pressing issue.

By the mid-Victorian period, central London could boast nearly two hundred gentlemen's clubs. Some, like the Trafalgar Cycling Club came and went very quickly but the prestigious establishments, mostly in or around Piccadilly and Pall Mall, had long waiting lists. Their appeal was described by Max Schlesinger, an Anglophile German writer who had settled in London. He enthused over:

> *... splendid carpets, sofas, arm-chairs, strong, soft, and roomy, in which a man might dream away his life; writing and reading-rooms tranquil enough to suit a poet, and yet*

*grand, imposing, aristocratic; doors covered with cloth to prevent the noise of their opening and shutting, and their brass handles resplendent as the purest gold; enormous fire-places surrounded by slabs of the whitest marble; the furniture of mahogany and palisander; the staircases broad and imposing as in the palazzos of Rome; the kitchens chefs d'oeuvre of modern architecture; bath and dressing-rooms got up with all the requirements of modern luxury; in short, the whole house full of comfortable splendour and substantial wealth.*

For young men, the club was a domestic convenience.

*A younger son of an old house, with an income of, say from two to four hundred pounds ... can neither take and furnish a house, nor can he keep a retinue of servants or give dinners to his friends. The club is his home. ... Dinners are good and cheap, compared to the extortionate prices of the London hotels.*

Complacency was the enemy. The all-male environment was conducive to a stolid traditionalism which offended livelier minds.

*It was not the thing to acknowledge anyone from a club window, whilst to raise the hat to a passing lady was a breach of club usage. The great majority of members lunched in the coffee-room with their hats on, whilst in certain clubs evening dress at dinner was practically compulsory. At one or two clubs ... a small apartment, separate*

> *from the regular dining-room, is reserved for members din-*
> *ing in day clothes. Smoking was strictly limited to certain*
> *rooms, usually the most uncomfortable, whilst strangers*
> *were, in many cases, only allowed in a small strangers'*
> *dining-room and the entrance hall.*

Old fogeys, deep in leather armchairs, grumbling over their brandy and sodas, set the tone for these 'monasteries of the married'.

> *When modern improvements were suggested, the old-*
> *fashioned members fought strenuously against them. The*
> *introduction of the electric light, for instance, was bit-*
> *terly opposed; whilst the telephone seemed to not a few of*
> *the older generation an attempt to introduce mercantile*
> *outposts into the very heart of clubland. The old club-men*
> *at first hated, and afterwards feared, the encroachments of*
> *business methods into their kingdom.*

At the end of the century, the *Westminster Gazette*, the thinking man's evening newspaper, put the question, 'Is club life doomed?' to which the answer was a resounding 'Yes'. The reasoning was based on the rise to popularity of the first class restaurant, animated, more amusing and in nine cases out of ten, offering meals that were more varied and better cooked than any that came out of a club kitchen.

The culinary revolution was led by French, Italian and German immigrants drawn to London's booming economy. The wealthy residents of Piccadilly were the key to the success for as-piring restaurateurs who found a ready market among those who were sick to death of 'plain English food'. It was all very well for

Lord Derby to proclaim the virtues of 'a small turbot, some well roasted lamb or duckling with green peas followed by a good apple or apricot tart', but the typical offering, for those who could afford it, leaned more towards over-cooked meat, boiled vegetables and milk puddings. The old fashioned chop houses and pubs serving scrag-ends had nothing to recommend them.

With the prestige restaurants came the restaurant critic with Lieut-Col Newnham-Davis as the first and foremost of his profession. After serving in the Zulu campaign of 1877-79 and in China and India, the gallant colonel retired from the army to profit from his favourite occupation which was to dine well in convivial company. As restaurant correspondent for the *Pall Mall Gazette*, his regular column followed a set pattern. He would invite a friend, invariably a lady disguised under a pseudonym, to join him for dinner at a restaurant of his choice. He did not limit himself to criticising the food, his guest for the evening could also expect a blunt appraisal. 'Miss Brighteyes' was a debutante who, shockingly, drank lemonade with her caviar and prattled about dresses and weddings while she ate *terrine de foie gras*. A more satisfactory companion for the Colonel was the American, 'Mrs Washington', who 'knows most people who are worth knowing in Europe and had been to most places worth seeing.' He decided to take her to Verrey's in Regent Street, a restaurant famous for providing a 'light' dinner for those going on to the theatre. This was the menu:

*Petite marmite*
*Oeufs à la Russe*
*Soufflé de filets de sole à la Verrey*

*Timbale Lucullus*
*Noisettes d'agneau à la Princesse*
*Petits pois à la Française*
*Pommes Mirelle*
*Aiguillettes de caneton à l'Orange*
*Salade Vénétienne*
*Pouding Saxon*
*Salade de fruits*

It is a tribute to the Victorian constitution that after such a feast anyone had the stamina to sit through a play.

The columns penned by Newnham-Davis reveal the staggering amount of food the rich put away day after day, every mouthful as much as their Georgian forebears. The table d'hôte at even a modest Soho restaurant offered at best five courses while in the better class places, ten course meals were not unusual. Though the Colonel was fond of his wine, champagne throughout dinner was generally the choice of his guests. It was ordered by the pint.

Though he could come across as a typical Victorian old fogey, Newnham-Davis had advanced views, not least on the right of women to drive independently without the company of a chaperone. His radicalism extended to clubland. He took the view that in competition with restaurants, clubs would not survive if they continued to shut their doors against women.

'By the end of the nineties the restaurant habit was a part of the capital's life,' wrote the journalist J.B. Booth. 'Old establishments had been refurbished, new ones were springing up with amazing rapidity; famous hoteliers, chefs and maîtres d'hôtel flocked to London ... a revolution had taken place in the habits and customs of London men and women.'

In 1885, Pascoe's guide to London felt safe to say, 'There is probably now no capital in Europe that can show so many spacious and splendid restaurants as London'.

Sandwich-board men marched the streets to promote the bills of fare with the dish of the day given special prominence. Among the restaurants that raised the stakes, the Berkeley on the corner of Piccadilly and Berkeley Street doubled its seating capacity while smartening up its image to increase business.

The Café Monico, which came to prominence on Piccadilly Circus, was a success story built on a shrewd property investment. In 1858 the Gatti brothers, Carlo and Giovanni, who sold ice cream and chocolates, set up in partnership with another recent immigrant, Giuseppe Monico, to buy up leases close to Hungerford Market. This put them in line for a handsome capital gain when, as confidently forecast, the Southeastern Railway Company extended its reach to Charing Cross. In today's money the gamble netted over a half million sterling.

Thus launched, the Gatti and Monico families spread their net to restaurants and music halls. When the partnership ended, Giuseppe's two sons opened the Café Monico at 15 Tichbourne Street. An advertisement on the back of a programme for the Argyll Rooms in 1878 promotes 'a grand café saloon ... grill room ... best ventilated billiard salon in London ... supper after the theatre and restaurant open till half past twelve'.

All was going well when in 1885 the Metropolitan Board of Works (MBW), the forerunner of the London County Council, announced that the Monico site was needed to make way for the new Shaftesbury Avenue to connect to Piccadilly Circus.

The brothers were right to be suspicious. The MBW had achieved much including the sewage system designed by Joseph Bazalgette, a brilliant civil engineer. But Board finances were dodgy. Notorious for accepting kickbacks, the members were known collectively, not without justice, as the Metropolitan Board of Perks.

What the Giuseppes had to go through to secure an alternative site is unknown. Suffice to say, a hundred year lease was secured on land covering the north east corner of the Circus, permitting the Café Monico to double in size. On its reopening, Newnham-Davis was keen to discover what the Monico had to offer. But first he was given a tour of the premises by the manager, Signor Giulio C. Nobile, 'a gentleman of stalwart figure with a pleasant smile and a small but carefully-tended moustache'.

> First we went into a great hall on the first floor, where a
> smoking-concert was in progress, and thunders of applause
> were greeting a gentleman in evening dress who had just
> concluded a song. 'It is someone going abroad, and they are
> giving him a send-off,' was Mr Nobile's explanation. Next
> we went down to the ground-floor through a hall, where
> people were sitting at little round-topped tables drinking
> various beverages, and down some steps into a German
> beer saloon with pigmies and other strange creatures
> painted on the walls. Up again to the first-floor, through a
> long grill-room with little white-clothed tables in four rows,
> then a peep into a restaurant, and a flight in the lift up to

*the second floor, where solemn gentlemen in black were
eating a dinner of ceremony in a very pretty saloon with
an Egyptian room as a reception-room next door. Our five
minutes were over, we had seen most of the big rooms of the
house, and, descending, we took our places at a table by one
of the windows in the Renaissance Saloon.*

The meal they enjoyed comprised:

*Hors-d'oeuvre variés
Consommé Bortsch
Crème à la Reine
Soles à la Nantua
Poularde Valencienne
Tournedos Princesse
Canards sauvages. Sauce Port wine
Salade
Biscuits Monico
Petit fours
Dessert*

Each dish was declared to be excellent in all respects but Newnham-Davis was left wondering if other guests had been treated so well.

The Café Monico was still in family hands after 1945 though soon afterwards austerity rationing and other restrictions persuaded the family to sell. In the 1970s, the Monico was demolished to make way for shops and snack-bars of unremitting ugliness. These too have now gone but whether the replacement will be an improvement has yet to be seen.

Strictly speaking, the Café Royal belongs to Regent Street but such is its social overlap with Piccadilly it comes within our remit. At the opening in 1865, few would have predicted its illustrious future. In fact, few would have predicted any future at all.

When Daniel Nicolas Thévenon, soon to Anglicise his name to Daniel Nicols, arrived in London he was on the run from French justice. After the financial collapse of his Parisian café venture, a long prison sentence had threatened. Exile was the alternative. Finding lodgings in Soho, Daniel made a living from casual work while his wife Célestine took to the needle and thread to supplement their meagre income.

But Daniel's ambitions to resume his occupation as a restaurateur was never far from sight. After less than two years of saving the pennies he was on the lookout for suitable premises. He found what he could afford in Glasshouse Street, not then the most salubrious neighbourhood but close on Regent Street with its select shops and moneyed patrons. Daniel's first customers were welcomed to what until recently had been a warehouse for selling oil cloth. The challenge was to rid the place of its pungent smell.

Daniel did not set out to attract the arty crowd. But in the curious and unfathomable way that haunts for writers and artists gain favour, the Café Royal with its distinctive red velvet seats was soon the meeting place of choice for the avant-garde. In short time Daniel expanded his premises into the adjoining property which gave him a Regent Street address. After 1867, 68 Regent Street was distinguished by a plate-glass window displaying tempting dishes on ornamental pedestals.

The layout of the Café Royal provided for a billiard room and wine cellar in the basement, a lunch bar at the front and a café to the rear with the kitchen and main restaurant on the first floor. On the upper floors were discreet private dining rooms where no questions were asked as to what went on behind closed doors.

> *With its marble top tables, there was nothing in the décor to make diners feel at home ... But there was nowhere else where one could find a microcosm that, conceivably on the same night, might have blended the verbal soufflés of Oscar Wilde with the nasal patter of bookmakers; the peacock screeches of Whistler with the prattle of models in second-hand pre-Raphaelite costumes; the boom and bluster of Frank Harris with the donnish and disdainful aperçus of A.E. Housman, and the hoarse whisper of con-men; the high-pitched brogue of George Bernard Shaw; the soft precision of Max Beerbohm, and the exquisite savagery of Aubrey Beardsley.*

Knowing his wine, Nicols stocked only the best. By the 1880s, Frank Harris, who never undersold his opinions, declared the Café Royal to 'have the best cellar in the world'. The restaurant was among the first to install electric light and to take reservations by telephone. The telegraphic address was simply Restaurant, London.

If it was Daniel who had the flair and imagination, he would have been lost without the practical common sense of his wife. Madame Célestine was always on hand to

*... see the waiters' shoes did not peer out from under their
long white aprons, that the many intricate brass fittings of the
establishment were polished till they sparkled, and that every
penny taken within that sprawling octopus of a building went
where it should go – par la caisse, and into the bank.*

The trappings of prosperity for Daniel and Célestine included a country estate with a deer park in Surbiton. The train into Waterloo put Nicols in easy reach of the Café Royal, as it did his son-in-law, Georges Pigache, whose enthusiastic attention to the kitchens made him a mega heavyweight in a profession given to over indulgence. At Surbiton railway station, it took three hefty porters to haul Georges into his carriage and to extract him on his return.

Concentrated on Soho and Piccadilly, the French colony in London numbered over eleven thousand. Their restaurants and shops satisfied a yearning for Gallic charm and taste, a light relief from Victorian starchiness. At the centre of the cultural crowd-puller was the Café Royal, the place to go said Sir Herbert Tree 'to see English people at their most English, trying their hardest to be French'.

From being the most famous of the Café Royal regulars, Oscar Wilde became the most infamous. His fall from grace marked a decline in Daniel Nichols's creation though he was not alive to see it. When he died in 1897, he left a fortune of £100,000 (about six million in today's money).

When the Regent Street Quadrant came to be rebuilt to accommodate the Piccadilly Hotel, the Café Royal with its four stout pillars and great oval medallion under a heavy balustrade, failed to pass the test of current architectural fashion. It was pulled down and rebuilt, reopening in 1928 with a banquet for five hundred guests. For those with long memories there was sadness in knowing that the 'artistic hot-air cupboard' had gone for good.

With the daily influx of shoppers and entertainment seekers, the way was open for mass catering. The inspiration for inexpensive restaurants serving wholesome food came from Australia where two English-born immigrants, Felix Spiers and Christopher Pond had launched a chain of refreshment venues. Encouraged by their success they decided to try their luck in the mother country. Their strategy was to site their restaurants where crowds gathered with time on their hands. Rail stations were their first target. So popular were their buffets and luncheon rooms, they soon branched out into more ambitious enterprises, hitting on the idea of building a theatre with a restaurant attached. They were not much interested in the drama as such. Rather, they anticipated that audiences would be attracted to an adjoining restaurant for a pre-performance meal or returning for supper after the curtain fell. An ideal site was on Piccadilly Circus where a place of entertainment known as the Piccadilly Dining Saloon was up for sale. What emerged in its place was the Criterion, now one of the most important surviving mid-Victorian theatres.

Architect Thomas Verity was commissioned to design a large restaurant with a linking theatre below street level, to be equipped with gas lighting. This was to cause problems with the licensing authority which, quite reasonably, feared for the safety of audiences ill-protected by inadequate ventilation. Electric lighting was installed ten years after the opening of the theatre in 1874.

Meanwhile, the Criterion restaurant, much larger than its latest incarnation, was a huge success with its East Room and Grill Room, both lavishly decorated (white gold and moss green for one, pink for the other), promoted as two of the most fashionable places to dine, accommodating between 2,000-4,000 covers a day. By contrast, the Long Bar was the meeting place for dubious characters known to the police as the 'Criterion Boys', being confidence men, card-sharps, racing tipsters and money lenders' touts. Spiers and Pond turned a blind eye to the source of what was a highly profitable business.

Where Spiers and Pound led, Joseph Lyons was not far behind. The firm was founded by Alfred Salmon and Montagu Gluckstein, whose fortune came from a chain of tobacconists and who now wanted to branch out into catering for trade exhibitions. Expansion into restaurants got them into partnership with Joseph Lyons. The son of an 'itinerant vendor of watches and cheap jewellery', with family links to the Glucksteins, Joe Lyons was the name that sounded a better fit with catering than that of émigré German Jews. The first venture was a teashop known as the Popular Café or The Pop, which opened at 213 Piccadilly in 1894 with seating for two hundred customers. It was an immediate success.

*Teas were marvellous at the Pop – you made a wonderful meal for a shilling, with a tremendous selection of cakes, and always an orchestra. A feature was that there were NO tips. I think that was more honoured in the breach than in the observance. But that was the rule. People from the suburbs and from the provinces flocked to the Pop. They*

*wore their best clothes and got a tremendous thrill out of*
*refreshing themselves in a marble hall in sacred Piccadilly.*
*What better after a tiring afternoon at the Royal Academy*
*in Burlington House than to pop into the Pop and get rid*
*of that headache the Academy always caused. The Pop was*
*a great example of business psychology. ... it was built on a*
*site previously occupied by the Geological Museum. Nobody*
*went to that. Everybody went to the Pop.*

Waitresses were young, single and slim.

By 1910, there were 150 Lyons teashops across central London. One step up was the Lyons Corner House. Making its debut in 1909 on Coventry Street, linking Piccadilly Circus with Leicester Square, the first corner house offered a more varied fare than the teashops. It was also on Coventry Street that Joe Lyons embarked on the company's most ambitious project to date. Built on the site of the Argyll Rooms, the new venue, a 'veritable palace of gastronomy,' had a spectacular marble staircase leading up to the dining area with its gallery and orchestra. At the lower level were smoking and billiard rooms, all lavishly furnished in the ornate Louis XV style.

The Lyons management strived for respectability. The Trocadero set out to appeal to the aspiring middle class who were liable to feel overwhelmed by, say, the Café Royal but were more at home in the less formal but nonetheless reassuringly warm surroundings favoured by Lyons.

*They approved the waiters – not in dirty stained old*
*evening clothes and 'dicky' fronts but resplendent attire,*

*with gold braided collars and well -trimmed side whiskers. The customers gasped at the scope and variety of the menu, and at the most reasonable prices, the quick silent service in luxurious surroundings and a wine list which provided superior drinking to the popular beer or spirits. Lyons had hit off the spirit of the age to perfection. Ladies could and did dine there unaccompanied by a gentleman and suffer no shame. Once, though, a rather worried but obliging management covered a lady in with screens because she insisted on smoking, elsewhere she would have been expelled.*

A strict code excluded those whose behaviour was deemed unacceptable. Staff were instructed on those to be turned away at the door. In the list for 1898:

*One of 'the Brothers Brown' was identified as a dangerous thief, the other as having 'no money to spend'. Ryley, Appletree, Fraser, and Piper had all served a term of imprisonment. Closer to home, a Mr Murray had apparently been 'drunk, [and] created a disturbance', as had someone identified (in an indication that Lyons' emphasis on self-discipline and probity applied across the social spectrum) as 'Rev. Young'. Someone called Townsend had been found fighting in the buffet, while George English used 'filthy expressions' in the same part of the restaurant. Other individuals were merely labelled as 'loafer' or 'undesirable', while Gordon Keyvett was deemed 'impossible to satisfy'.*

# 9

# Piccadilly Politicians

Elevated to the senior peerage and fresh from his triumph at Waterloo, the Duke of Wellington was showered with more medals and awards than he could pin across his chest. A grateful nation awarded him a country estate of his choice. He settled on the five thousand acres surrounding Stratfield Saye House in Hampshire for £263,000 less than half the amount voted by Parliament.

There was little in its favour, one visitor describing it as a 'miserable imitation of a French château' and another as 'damp and low'. They were more impressed by his London residence, Apsley House, now a museum dedicated to Wellingtonia.

Apsley House at Hyde Park Corner was known as No.1 London since it was the first house after the tall gates at the top of the road from Knightsbridge. Equally, it could be singled out as No.1 Piccadilly. Wellington bought the house from his brother Richard who needed the money. Built between 1771 and 1778 by Robert Adam on the site of the Hercules Pillars tavern, it was first occupied by Lord Apsley – reckoned to be the laziest and most incompetent Lord Chancellor of the eighteenth century – until it passed to Wellington's elder sibling.

Apsley House, home of the Duke of Wellington, known as No.1 London

Altered substantially before the Duke moved in, an extension from 1819 allowed for a state dining room with additional bedrooms and dressing rooms. By contrast, Wellington's bedroom, seen today much as he left it, was a simple apartment on the ground floor. Later changes included a new staircase and the Waterloo Gallery where the annual Waterloo banquet was held for up to seventy-four guests.

The furnishings were enriched by a collection of pictures from Spanish palaces. Purloined by Napoleon's brother, Joseph, they fell into Wellington's hands at the battle of Vitoria. When King Ferdinand was restored to the Spanish throne, the Duke was ready to return the pictures but Ferdinand would have none of them. He was content that the art should remain at Apsley House in recognition of Wellington's service to the royal house.

Appreciative though he may have been (who would not have taken pride in a Velasquez or Correggio on display?), the Iron Duke's taste in art was more protean. While he bought paintings of the Dutch school and other Old Masters, he liked to be reminded of his great days as a military commander.

He paid what was then thought to be an enormous fee of £1,260 to David Wilkie for his depiction of *Chelsea Pensioners Reading the Gazette of the Battle of Waterloo*. He spent a similar amount on the purchase of Sir William Allan's painting of *The Battle of Waterloo from the English Side*, displayed at the Scotch Academy exhibition of 1843. When it came to paying Allan, the artist found him carefully counting out the sum in bank notes. Allan suggested that a cheque would save time and trouble. The response from Wellington: 'Do you suppose I am going to let Coutts people know what a damned fool I've been?'.

Wellington was famed for his laconic responses to over-eager questioners. When asked what Waterloo was like, all he would say was, 'Damned hot while it lasted.'

In the hall at Apsley House stood Canova's huge nude statue of Napoleon, unsurprisingly rejected by the Emperor. It was stored at the Louvre until bought by the British government to be presented to Wellington.

Opposite Apsley House on Hyde Park Corner was the Wellington Arch which served as the pedestal for a colossal bronze statue of Wellington astride a horse, the first equestrian statue of a person other than a monarch to be erected in London. Modelled by Matthew Cotes Wyatt and his son, James, this monster of 40 tons, measuring twenty-six feet nose to tail and thirty feet high was large enough to accommodate a party of twelve who dined in it the day before it was placed in position.

Apart from the Duke, no one was other than appalled by the statue. Queen Victoria called it 'a perfect disgrace' and expressed the wish that it should be 'covered over and hidden from sight'. But it stayed in place during Wellington's lifetime. A decision on its future was delayed until 1883 when Decimus Burton's much praised Wellington Arch (now the Constitution Arch) was moved to its present position on the axis of Constitution Hill. Taken from its plinth, Wellington immortalised in bronze was carted off to Aldershot where it was allowed to rust until restored by local conservationists.

With his unrivalled status it was inevitable that Wellington should be drawn into high level politics. But the transition was not easy. Used to getting results by command, he was instinctively opposed to democracy. An apocryphal story has Wellington as prime minister (1828-29), emerging from a cabinet meeting in thoroughly disgruntled mood. Asked why, he complained, 'I gave them my orders and they wanted to discuss them.'

The underlying truth illustrates Wellington's frustration at having to hold together a fragile Tory coalition opposed to change in the face of a determined Whig-led demand for electoral reform. To add to his troubles, his wife, cared for at Apsley House, was close to death. It had not been a happy marriage. The Duchess, shy and short-sighted, unable to cope with household management and often sick, was overwhelmed by Wellington's outsized personality. Spending most of her time at Stratfield Saye while the Duke remained in London, it was only at the end that there was a reconciliation with Wellington sitting for hours by her bedside. She died on April 24th, 1831.

By this time, a government led by Lord Grey, the same Lord Grey who had sowed his wild oats with Georgiana, Duchess of Devonshire, had introduced into the House of Commons a Reform Bill to extend the franchise and to change constituency boundaries to make for fairer representation. The Bill was passed by the House of Commons but subsequently rejected by the Lords. Rioting across the country reached a pitch in London where Wellington took the brunt of the attack. An effigy of the Duke was burned at Tyburn and Apsley House was stoned by a mob. The windows were protected by metal grills, the shutters closed on the ground floor and armed men posted in the garden.

The riots confirmed Wellington's worst fears of a country beholden to the lower orders. They are 'rotten to the core', he told Harriet Arbuthnot, his closest female friend. And to Harriet's husband, Charles, he argued that it was a great mistake to educate the common people. 'They want to resort to our private houses, our entertainment, have the run of our kitchens and dance with our wives and daughters.' But ever the practical strategist, Wellington recognised compromise as the only means of staving off a revolution. Having failed to put together a government capable of resisting Grey, he accepted reforms with the proviso 'the more gentle and more gradual, the better'. The Reform Bill became law on June 7th, 1832.

Wellington had no shortage of female admirers and while not immune to their charms, he found them, for the most part, surplus to his bachelor life. There were two exceptions. Harriet Arbuthnot was as close to him as any one person was likely to get. When she died of cholera in 1834, he was bereft, sharing the grief of Harriet's husband who told Wellington, 'You never had such a friend before and you will never have such a one again.' To retain the link, Wellington suggested to Charles Arbuthnot that he should move to Apsley House. He was there for the rest of his life.

The other woman in Wellington's life we met earlier. A nearby neighbour in Piccadilly, Angela Burdett-Coutts had everything in life except someone to share her enormous wealth and the responsibilities that came with it. In her frequent meetings with Wellington she fastened on to a father figure who could offer advice without any ulterior motive. Angela was not inclined to take seriously his objections to her philanthropic enterprises though his scepticism that charity encouraged idleness may have restrained some of her more ambitious schemes.

A turning point in their relationship came in 1847 when the 32-year-old shy and reserved Angela plucked up courage to ask the 77-year-old Duke to marry her. Having survived three strokes, Wellington suffered rheumatism and deafness which made him a social liability except for those who knew him too well to care. But in Angela's company, he came alive. Even so, however tempted, he was too much of a realist to allow Angela to put herself in an impossible position. In writing to decline her offer of marriage, Wellington revealed a softer, more sympathetic side of his character that rarely surfaced.

*My dearest Angela, I have passed every Moment of the Evening and Night since I quitted you in reflecting upon our conversation of yesterday. Every Word of which I have considered repeatedly. My first Duty towards you is that of Friend, Guardian, Protector. You are Young, My Dearest! You have before you the prospect of at least twenty years of enjoyment of Happiness in Life. I entreat you again in this way not to throw yourself upon a Man old enough to be your Grandfather, who, however strong, Hearty and Healthy at present, must and will certainly in time feel the consequences and Infirmities of Age. You cannot know, but I do, the dismal consequences to you of this certainty.*

*My last days would be embittered by the reflection that your Life was uncomfortable and hopeless. God Bless you my Dearest!*

They remained the closest of friends. When Wellington died, in 1852, Angela was at the funeral alongside the ladies of the family. It was a state affair with a lengthy lying in state before the huge funeral carriage, drawn by twelve horses led the slow procession to St Paul's Cathedral. Such was the weight of the carriage (now at Stratfield Saye) that Berry Brothers, the old-established wine and spirit merchants in St James's Street, reinforced its cellars under the road for fear of a breakthrough.

The mob violence of the 1830s long forgotten, Wellington was anointed 'the greatest Englishman' by Poet Laureate Alfred Lord Tennyson. His judgement was confirmed by general acclaim.

꙳

No one knew quite what to make of Henry Brougham. A principal campaigner for Parliamentary reform and for the abolition of slavery, his brilliance was undeniable. But such was his force of character, he was liable to overwhelm enemies and friends alike, hardly pausing to distinguish between the two.

When he stormed into Albany in 1806 he was just twenty-eight, a product of the Scottish middle class who made no secret of his ambition. As a co-founder with Sidney Smith of *The Edinburgh Review*, he was already known as an acerbic critic. Had he been more circumspect, he might have thought twice before taking on Lord Byron. But Brougham never fought shy of a battle. Having choked over *Hours of Idleness*, Byron's first published volume of poems, Brougham did not hold back: 'The reader must be content with these adolescent efforts ... for they are the last we shall ever hear from him.'

Byron's response was to lash out in all directions with his lengthy verse satire, *English Bards and Scotch Reviewers*. It was fortunate that Brougham and Byron did not overlap in Albany.

Brougham's rise through the political ranks was assisted by his appearance, not so much distinguished as distinguishable. A lanky figure with crumpled features and a large fleshy nose, he was a caricaturist's dream. Disrespectful appearances in *Punch* supported the mantra that there is no such thing as bad publicity.

Elected in 1810 to represent Camelford in the House of Commons, he threw himself into the campaign for reforming the franchise, the abolition of slavery, an end to ecclesiastical abuses that favoured the higher clergy and for universal education. His voice in the Commons was augmented by articles in *The Times* where his radicalism found favour with Thomas Barnes, a reforming editor.

By 1830, Brougham was widely touted as the most single dynamic force in politics. Though exceptional in having no aristocratic antecedents, Lord Grey felt compelled to give him high office, making him Lord Chancellor in his reform ministry. He soon regretted it. Fuelled by heavy doses of laudanum and alcohol, Brougham embarked on a wholesale clear-out of a legal system that permitted its leading lights to extract extortionate fees while turning aside cases of blatant injustice.

If his achievements fell short, Brougham can take credit for setting in train a wholesale reform of the law while establishing the Central Criminal Court and extending the powers of the Judicial Committee of the Privy Council as a Court of Appeal. How his traditionally inclined colleagues – reform but not yet – hated him.

When Lord Melbourne succeeded to the premiership in 1834, he retained Brougham as Lord Chancellor but by the time he formed his second government a year later, he took the opportunity to rid himself of his troublesome colleague. Demanding an explanation for his dismissal, Melbourne was delighted to give it.

*I will tell you fairly, that, in my opinion, you domineered too much, you interfered too much with other departments, you encroached upon the provinces of the Prime Minister, you worked, as I believe, with the Press in a manner unbecoming to the dignity of your station, and you formed political views of your own and pursued them by means which were unfair towards your colleagues.*

And that was that. Though he remained active in the House of Lords for the next thirty years, Brougham was never to regain office. His restless energy found its reward outside politics. It was Brougham who designed the four-wheeled carriage named after him. And it was Brougham who trail-blazed the Riviera as a holiday destination. Interrupting a journey with a stay in the little fishing village of Cannes, he was so taken with its charm, he bought a plot of land to build a villa. It was the start of the British migration to escape Fog-land as he called England. Brougham died in Cannes at the age of 89 in 1868. There remains a statue of him on the promenade.

৵৵

There were high hopes for the young man who took up residency in Albany in March 1833. Three months earlier, a few days before his twenty-third birthday, William Ewart Gladstone had been elected to Parliament. His patron, the Duke of Newcastle, had spent a small fortune slotting him into Newark where he was one of two Tory members. But his chief gratitude was to his father, a Liverpool businessman who provided William with a comfortable income and paid for his London accommodation. His thanks were profuse.

> *I am getting on rapidly with my furnishing and I shall be able, I feel confident, to do it all, including plate, within the liberal limits which you allow. I cannot warmly enough thank you for the terms and footing on which you propose to place me in the chambers, but I really fear that after this year my allowance in all will be greater not only than I have any title to, but than I ought to accept without blushing.*

With his Oxford double first in classics and mathematics, his talent for marshalling arguments that defied contradiction and an enthusiasm for political debate, William's ascent to government was seemingly assured. If confirmation was needed it came in 1835 when, briefly, he was appointed Under Secretary of State for the Colonies in a short-lived Tory government led by Sir Robert Peel.

But the way forward was not entirely obstacle free. His nature was introspective and while many of his generation agonised over reconciling Christian doctrine with the compromises of everyday life, the young Gladstone was more than averagely given to dark thoughts about mortal sin and his own capacity for keeping it at bay.

It was a preoccupation that dampened his social life and, in politics, set him apart from those of a more pragmatic turn of mind. An immediate challenge was the battle between his conscience and what he called the 'burdensome question' hovering over the family fortune. His father, John Gladstone, had made the bulk of his money by branching out from the corn trade to owning plantations of sugar and coffee in the West Indies. It was a prosperity based on slavery.

John Gladstone, himself an MP from 1818 to 1827 when he was unseated for bribery, was in frequent and acrimonious dispute with the abolitionists, notably after an insurrection on his properties in Demerara was put down savagely in 1823. One of the victims was a white missionary, John Smith, who was found guilty of complicity and sentenced to death. Before the judgement could be overturned, he died of consumption.

John Gladstone's cultured image was of a devout Christian, a generous benefactor of good causes. But when it came to his own best interests, he was a hard man who spoke out passionately in defence of the West Indian planters. Slavery, according to the elder Gladstone, was sanctioned by God as an antidote to the indolence of the natives in tropical climes. He pitched into missionaries as revolutionary agents while telling his critics at home that if they were so concerned with the public wellbeing, they might do more for the oppressed workers on their doorstep.

Whatever the doubts harboured by William, his devotion to his father was paramount. Thus we have the paradox of a politician who was to achieve immortality as the upholder of human rights and champion of the underdog, starting his career by defending his father's record as an unenlightened plantation owner.

In his comfortable surroundings in Albany, paid for by slave labour nearly four thousand miles away, Gladstone spent many hours trying to balance family loyalty with his commitment to the equality of man. In later life he professed always to have believed that slavery was 'evil and demoralising'. But in 1833, when he devoted his first major Commons speech to the subject, he settled for emancipation but not yet, arguing that only after a lengthy period of moral education would slaves be ready to lead independent lives. In practical terms, he did little to help the slaves. At one point, he announced he would follow the example of Mathew Lewis by inspecting at first hand conditions on the family plantations. His father put a stop to that.

With the extension of the franchise to the middle class in 1832, there was a Commons majority for the abolition of slavery throughout the British Empire. But the Emancipation Bill that became law in August 1804 accepted that slave owners had to be compensated for the loss of what was commonly regarded as their property. It was an argument fully supported by the young Gladstone.

The pay-out amounted to twenty million pounds, no less than forty per cent of the government's annual spending. Some £375,000 went to the Gladstone family. There was never any suggestion of compensating eight hundred thousand slaves for their years of subjection.

While the Gladstones eventually made their peace with the abolitionists, William continued to defend the West Indian planters. In March, 1838, he spoke in the Commons for two hours opposing a motion to cut by two years the period of compulsory apprenticeship that had been introduced as a condition of abolition. He did not get his way. The apprenticeship system was soon abolished.

In his first two decades as a Member of Parliament, Gladstone made more speeches on slavery than on any other subject. Yet his biographers have given little or no attention to his struggle to square the circle or acknowledge that during his early political life he was financially dependent on his father. Though he came to deny the right of the white man to keep the black in subjection, he continued to believe that blacks, along with other non-Europeans, were 'a race of lower capacities'.

Can anything be said in defence of Gladstone's stance on slavery? Care must be taken in attributing blame for actions and attitudes adopted when life was very different. Women and children who were exploited shamelessly in the coal mines and textile mills suffered a subjection every bit as harsh as those who worked the sugar plantations. Life expectancy for slaves in British West Indies was actually higher than that for industrial workers in Lancashire and Yorkshire.

But the principle of one person owning another as property to be bought, sold and constrained under a prison regime was beyond question wrong. And Gladstone, in his heart, knew it.

꣠꣠

Though Viscount Palmerston, twice prime minister, came late to marriage he was no stranger to sharing a bed. As a young man, with a chubby face, curly red hair and a roguish eye, he was known as Lord Cupid, 'a devil among the ladies'. When his reputation for romantic escapades was at its height, Lady Shaftesbury upbraided him for paying too much attention to young married women: 'To begin with, it is wrong' secondly, it is ungentlemanlike; and lastly, it is stupid for it can never succeed.' Palmerston was quick to respond:

'Madam, as regards the religious aspect, I doubt the practice of the Churches differs. The taste is a matter of opinion – I think it is most gentlemanlike. As to the results, however, your Ladyship is misinformed, for I have never known to fail.' At age seventy-nine he was taken to court for allegedly seducing a journalist's wife.

Palmerston was fifty-five and had been prominent in politics for thirty years when he married Emily, widow of the 5th Earl Cowper. She was then aged fifty-two and had known Palmerston for some time as a friend and, latterly, as her lover, a welcome relief from her dull and withdrawn husband.

After a decent interval following the death of Lord Cowper and two days into the reign of Queen Victoria, the couple made their vows. Home was Broadlands, a Palladian style mansion in Hampshire and later Cambridge House, 94 Piccadilly. The one-time home of the Egremonts, the house had been occupied by the Duke of Cambridge. On his death in 1850, Cambridge House passed to Sir Richard Sutton, one of the county's wealthiest men, who was ground landlord for much of Piccadilly. It was shortly after his death that the house was sold to Lord Palmerston.

Palmerston was close to the peak of an illustrious career. Beginning as a Junior Lord of the Admiralty in 1807, he had been Secretary at War under successive Tory prime ministers from 1809 to 1828. From 1830 to 1841 he was Foreign Secretary and again from 1846 to 1851.

Holding office at the height of Britain's imperial power, Palmerston was John Bull incarnate, a stout defender of national interests who was more popular at home than abroad. But while he could be accused of bullying lesser nations, he worked constructively to maintain the European balance of power and to keep the peace.

His path to the premiership, which he gained in 1855, was eased by Lady Palmerston whose social and diplomatic skills helped clear the way of obstacles to his advancement. As the sister of Lord Melbourne, Emily was experienced enough in politics to know the value of a good party. Invitations to weekend gatherings at No. 94 were greatly prized. Guests were received at the top of the staircase by the last of the great Piccadilly hostess, flashing diamonds and resplendent in fashionable crinolines. Not all the arrivals were natural allies of her husband. But Emily made no distinction between friends and rivals, her assumption being that courtesy and generosity could overcome all prejudices. Eyes were raised when journalists were invited. Casting a critical eye over the guest lists, Queen Victoria tried to persuade Palmerston to exclude hacks who had criticised the royal family. Quite impossible, said the prime minister, though he conceded that the profession was 'not yet considered to be entirely respectable'.

Palmerston's relations with the Queen were not easy. A mercurial personality who did not bear fools gladly, he found royal intrusion into affairs of state unwarranted and unhelpful. Lady Palmerston urged tact, telling her husband that he contradicted the Queen's notions 'too boldly'.

*I am sure it would be better if you said less to her – even if you act as you think best. ... You always think you can convince people by Arguments. ... All the explanations you give only prove to her how deeply imbued you are with*

*what she calls error, & how impossible it is for her to make*
*any effect on you. I should treat what she says more lightly*
*& courteously, and not enter into argument with her, but*
*lead her on gently, by letting her believe you have both the*
*same opinions in fact & the same wishes, but take some-*
*times different ways of carrying them out.*

This wise advice adopted by Palmerston in so far as he was able eased relations with the Palace. In 1856, the Queen awarded her prime minister with the Order of the Garter as a token of her approval of his 'zealous and able' conduct of affairs.

It was during Palmerston's time at Cambridge House that it was given two gates, one marked IN, the other OUT. With the stream of carriages lining up in Piccadilly, there was certainly a need for traffic management.

Into his final years, Palmerston lost none of his energy and sheer exuberance. Asked why he deliberately sought discomfort by writing his letters standing at a high desk, he said he had so much correspondence, if he sat down to deal with it, he would fall asleep. More probably, he was intent on demonstrating that he was immune to the penalties of old age. A keen horseman, he was the last prime minister to ride to Parliament.

❧❧

Albany was the perfect setting for Thomas Babington Macaulay. An obsessive workaholic, he sought peace and solitude in congenial surroundings where he could pursue his mission to fill 'a great void' by writing a history of England from the Glorious Revolution of 1688 to modern times.

'I have taken a very comfortable suite of chambers in the Albany,' he wrote to a friend on July 12th, 1841, 'and I hope to lead, during some years, a sort of life peculiarly suited to my taste, - college life at the West-end of London. I have an entrance hall, two sitting-rooms, a bed-room, a kitchen, cellars and two rooms for servants, - all for ninety guineas a year; and this in a situation which no younger son of a Duke need be ashamed to put on his card.'

As described by his brother-in-law, Charles Trevelyan, 'His chambers, every corner of which was library, were comfortably, though not very brightly, furnished. The ornaments were few, but choice – half a dozen fine Italian engravings from his favourite masters; a handsome French clock, provided with a singularly melodious set of chimes, the gift of his friend and publisher, Mr Thomas Longman; and the well-known bronze statuettes of Voltaire and Rousseau (neither of them heroes of his own), which had been presented to him by Lady Holland as a remembrance of her husband.'

The scale of Macaulay's ambition must be set in the context of a national culture that had given little attention to the past. To close on the end of the nineteenth century, hardly any history, outside the classics, was taught, even in the leading schools. Macaulay was to change that. Moreover, he was to give history a cachet that made it popular for the general reader.

He was well suited to his task. Blessed with a photographic memory, he was unsurpassed at clearing through a mass of material to find the core of an argument. After graduating from Trinity College, Cambridge, he was soon picked out for a political future.

Within two years of his election to the House of Commons, he was made Secretary to the Board of Control for India. Here was the opportunity for him to take a central role in developing a civil administration for India where the commercial wings of the East India Company were in urgent need of clipping.

In 1833, Macaulay was offered a seat on the newly created Supreme Council for India. The appointment came with an eye-watering salary of £10,000 a year (roughly £400,000 in today's money) for five years. Seizing the opportunity to acquire the security for a literary life, he departed for India where he set his mind to devising a criminal code and to founding an education system with English as the language of instruction.

On his return home, for two years he was Secretary for War in Lord Melbourne's ministry and for a few months in 1846-47, Paymaster of the Forces. But with his defeat in his Edinburgh constituency, he abandoned politics to devote his energies to his great work. Published in November 1848, the first two volumes of *Macaulay's History*, carrying the story to the overthrow of James II, were immediate bestsellers. The third and fourth volumes, published in 1855, enjoyed even greater success, selling 26,500 copies in ten weeks.

The secret of Macaulay's success was partly his skill in putting across a good story. But he also had the advantage of saying what people, not least the political elite, wanted to hear. Imbued with the romanticism of Walter Scott's historical novels, Macaulay provided comfort in his sure knowledge that Britain was best in all things and that the future was bright.

With hindsight, there was much to fault in Macaulay's interpretation of history with his emphasis on the contribution of great men, never women; his ignorance of art, architecture and music (though this did not deter him from dogmatic judgements) and his disdain for political theory and theorists who, lacking direct political experience, put their faith in 'paper constitutions'.

Macaulay was in favour of extending the franchise but only so far as to take in the middle class, 'that, brave, honest and sound-hearted class, which is as anxious for the maintenance of order and security of property as it is hostile to corruption and oppression'. Who, among his readers, could not say amen to that?

Mesmerised by his charitable view of middle class values while ignoring the distortion of self-interest, Macaulay had no feel for the social malaise caused by the industrial revolution.

His devotion to work took its toll. After suffering a heart attack in 1852, he accepted a peerage and gave up his apartment in Albany to move to a spacious villa in Kensington. When he died in December 1859, the fifth volume of his History had still to be completed. Edited by his sister, it appeared in 1861.

Alone among the former residents of Albany, Macaulay has a commemorative plaque. He is also remembered by the iron gates protecting the Savile Row end of Albany. These were erected after Macaulay was fooled into believing an anonymous warning, supposedly from one of a gang of thieves, of an imminent nocturnal break-in. The practical joker, a niece, eventually confessed but the gates remained.

# 10
# Street Life

*'The Nineties were not only jolly but truly wonderful, the peak years of that British prosperity which commenced in 1850 when the Income Tax was only eight pence in the pound, years when everybody lived happy and content in comfort and security.'*

So said actor Seymour Hicks whose theatrical stardom put him in the bracket of high earners. Most of his fellow citizens were less fortunate. Piccadilly was a magnet for the camp followers of the wealthy. Beggars were easily recognisable though hardly popular characters. One went by the name of Jane Cakebread. Her claim to fame was her professional longevity and the number of her convictions, well over a hundred, for drunkenness and uproarious behaviour.

The journalist J.B. Booth recalled a Darby and Joan he knew well by sight.

A bustling Piccadilly Circus in the late 19th century

*They were getting on in years; they were picturesque – at a distance – and one was 'Totally Blind from Birth'. This sad fact was announced on a placard worn round the neck. They took it in turns to wear the placard. A quarrel arose one day, apparently as to whose rightful turn it was to be totally blind. I heard part of it. However weak their eye-*

*sight, it was more than compensated for by their immense command of strong language.*

Street vendors competed volubly to scratch a marginal living. The loud ringing of a hand bell announced the imminence of the muffin-man. On his head he balanced a baize-lined tray covered with a white cloth. His uniform was a white apron. 'How he managed it I cannot tell, but he always seemed to pass the house at the most appropriate time. Where he came from no man knew, and whither he went was an equal mystery.'

A close rival was the potato-man. His stock in trade was a wheeled store.

*It was seen to great advantage on a cold, snowy night. The red glow from the fire was reflected on the white surface of the snow, and hot cinders hissed as they fell through the grill.*

*As customer after customer presented himself it was a sight to watch the merchant select the potato he deemed best done, and to see how dexterously he broke it open, showing the floury contents steaming in the frozen air. For a small extra charge you had a 'dab' of butter thrown in. The salt he sprinkled on 'free'.*

*'All 'ot! All 'ot' was the cry.*

Also hot were the chestnuts roasted over burning coals. The sellers wore woollen mufflers – 'long, thick and filthy'. Every trader had his own distinctive dress. Milkmen wore straw hats while butchers had their striped aprons. Shoeblacks sported red coats and carried with them a box containing polish and brushes which also served as a raised surface for customers to plant a foot. 'Shine, sir? Only a penny, shine, sir?'

Coalmen wore leather hats with a flap at the back to protect the neck against the heavy sacks they had to carry while draymen delivering beer had baize coats and red flannel caps. Bystanders gathered to watch them handle barrels with an ease that came with life-long practice. Costermongers selling fruit and vegetables from painted donkey-carts were identified by their bell-bottomed trousers, large neckerchiefs and, invariably, high-waisted pearl-decorated jackets. The women favoured large hats adorned with ostrich feathers and lace-up boots reaching far up the leg.

> *Their life was one incessant fight against bad weather, police regulations, and tradesmen who resented their competition, but when they died they went to the grave in a blaze of glory, with silver and black hearses, sable plumes, five or six coaches of principal mourners, and ten to twenty donkey barrows bearing their pals of the market place where, in their prime, they had shouted 'Fine almond celery, and fresh boiled beetroots!'*

The bank and office clerks, celebrated in *Diary of a Nobody*, turned out in black coat and pin-striped trousers, the uniform of the aspiring middle class. They were a cut above the skilled craftsmen in their blue overalls. Ordinary labourers had a special kind of jacket with capacious pockets and corduroy trousers, fastened at the knee with a leather strap. On the lowest scale:

*There were vendors of watercress, shrimps and winkles, without whose wares no Sunday tea-table was then complete. There was the groundsel-seller who has gone completely from the London scene. The one I remember was a poor old fellow of about seventy, who looked as if he had been born in a ditch, was living in a ditch, and would undoubtedly die in a ditch. His little bundles of groundsel, which he gathered himself in the surrounding fields, were neatly packed in a rush basket, and he sold them (when he was lucky) for a halfpenny a bundle.*

Street entertainers were on every corner.

*A familiar feature of the West End was generally to be seen of an evening at the corner of Suffolk Street, off the Haymarket, where used to stand a man with a large cage on wheels, which contained canaries, white mice, and cats, all living together in perfect friendliness. The canaries and the white mice performed tricks on a wire or a pole, and the cats gave a boxing performance.*

Children were diverted by Punch and Judy booths with the hidden puppeteer dispensing sadism with menacing high-pitched cries that never ceased to captivate a young audience.

Organ-grinders were invariably Italians with flashing teeth and curled moustaches while German bands, sporting tight-fitting military uniforms to perform favourite tunes from Viennese operettas were much missed when, come the Great War, they disappeared leaving behind a sad refrain:

*Has anyone seen a German band,*
*German band,*
*German band,*
*I've looked everywhere both near and far,*
*Near and far,*
*Ja, Ja, Ja,*
*But I miss my Fritz*
*What plays twiddley-bits*
*On the big trombone.*

Other musical performers fondly recalled range from a dignified old lady who sang *Just a Song at Twilight* to harp accompaniment to a virtuoso who played the *Light Cavalry Overture* on glasses suspended from a wooden frame.

The philosopher of Piccadilly was the coffee-stall proprietor.

*Upon nails on his walls he hung cups and mugs and jugs. From the cavities of the magic chest a stove was produced and lighted, and in the coffee-urn above it the coffee was soon hissing and steaming. From unsuspected corners the bustling proprietor hauled out rich-looking cakes, fresh loaves, and pats of butter. Tins of milk appeared from the depths, and the business of the night began. The characters that came to him as customers would have set up half a dozen novelists. There were tragedy and comedy around him night after night to have made the fortune of an observant playwright.*

Street traders and pedestrians alike were in competition with the traffic. Before Piccadilly was widened around the turn of the century, the street was jammed with private and public conveyances. There were no rules of the road to be observed and no policemen on point duty. Every driver of a horse-drawn vehicle had the inalienable right to pull up and park wherever he chose. An unnamed soldier, a bearer of the Victoria Cross, was quoted as saying that the bravest thing he had ever done was to cross Piccadilly Circus.

Defying the odds, the First Earl of Londesborough persisted in driving his four-in-hand through Piccadilly on his way to the Mall.

> *One of the most popular sporting noblemen of the period,*
> *he was content to handle the ribbons without attempting to*
> *cut a dash of any kind. The livery of his grooms, however,*
> *added a welcome splash of colour to the varied scene, and*
> *the sound of the coach horn which heralded the approach of*
> *his leaders added music to the rattling of burnished chains*
> *and the clatter of iron shoes which struck sparks from flint*
> *and paving-stones. It was no mean achievement to steer*
> *high-spirited animals through a veritable maze of vehicles,*
> *but this His Lordship did with the greatest possible ease.*

While shopping for essentials was delegated to servants, the purchase of luxuries was a social performance of great élan.

> *In Piccadilly, shopping was shopping de luxe. The gleaming*
> *carriage and high-spirited horses pulled up at the entrance,*
> *the coachman sat rigidly at attention, the piquer jumped*
> *nimbly down and opened the carriage door with a flourish.*

*First he removed the opulent rugs that were essential to protect the precious burden from the rude breath of Boreas, then he stood aside, holding the door open with one hand and bearing the rugs over his unoccupied arm, an incredible figure viewed in the light of to-day, with his spotless fawn coat, top boots, white doeskin breeches and top hat decorated with a cockade. My lord and lady then alighted and sailed across the pavement to the obsequious doorman who swung open the door for them to enter. If the weather was wet the doorman advanced with a huge umbrella to escort them across the pavement, and he also carried a curved wicker protector to place over the carriage wheel in case my lady's voluminous dress should be fouled by contact with it while alighting.*

Working horses of humble ownership were not well treated. Living at the corner of Charles Street, Lady Clodagh Anson 'could not look out of the window or move out of the door without seeing the incessant struggling and slithering of horses on wet, muddy days. Lots of the streets were paved with stone cobbles, and the clatter and falling of horses perpetually went on. I don't suppose we ever went for a walk as children without seeing two or three horses down, and the first thing one did as a matter of course was to go and sit on their heads to keep them from struggling until the harness had been undone or cut, and the cart moved back, so that they could get up by themselves without breaking their back or legs against the pole shafts.

Lady Clodagh deplored 'the misery of driving behind lame or tired horses, and having to stand the eternal thrashing of them that went on the whole time – to see the wretched bus-horses straining and sweating to get up the hills, or even to start at all.'

Everywhere there was the all-pervading stink of horse dung, only slightly mitigated by the efforts of freelance sweepers to clear the street crossings.

> *There was an old woman who swept a crossing in St James's*
> *Square, and she fed all the cats in the district. She had a*
> *little camp-stool by the railings of the Square garden, and*
> *sat there surrounded by cats. We knew her very well, and*
> *she always said: 'Good morning, my lady,' when we went by.*

Boys who took to sweeping for penny tips were seen off by the regulars who relied on the generosity of local householders.

> *There was, for example, a picturesque character, a rubi-*
> *cund, portly old boy, a standing advertisement for good ale,*
> *who, dressed in shabby hunting pink, with the hunting-cap*
> *of the shires, swept one of the crossings in Pall Mall. ... He*
> *seemed to derive quite an enviable competence from the old*
> *clubmen who used his crossing. Another sweeper who made*
> *an attempt at respectability, 'dressed like a country woman,*
> *always wore a clean white apron and knitted in her leisure*
> *hours, which were many'.*

Animals, not all domesticated, were left free to scavenge. The star of Piccadilly was a large white goat, a friendly creature but not one to allow liberties. Those who got too close were liable to be butted, albeit gently.

*It was wont to wander, pensive and unattended, along this old street, in which it was so perfectly at home, stopping occasionally to browse on such railings as, in spite of many former ineffectual attacks, seemed likely to afford some promise of refreshment.*

*From time to time, when wearied with its ill-success in this direction, it would wander into clubs. In the hall of one of them it ate up the tape; at another it walked upstairs into the coffee-room, where it created a stampede.*

The goat was well connected. It belonged to the Rothschilds and had its quarters in a stable off Stratton Street.

Buses or omnibuses, as they were called then, were each pulled by two horses.

*The driver was usually a very cheery chap, with a rubi-cund face – for he was exposed to all weathers – and pretty smartly dressed. Some of them wore toppers made of felt – some actual silk toppers – rather the worse for wear – and a large proportion wore bowlers. They sat well tucked up on their driving seat high above their horses with many rugs around their knees and up to their waists.*

They worked up to fourteen hours a day.

Passenger seating was either 'knife-board', long benches par-allel to the sides of the bus or 'garden' with seats designed for two, placed one behind the other and divided by an aisle down the centre. The upper deck was open to the sky.

The conductor with his packet of tickets and hand punch, started and stopped the bus by pulling a thin cord or by stamping on the floor or just by calling out to the driver. Rival companies fought hard for custom. With no Stop by Request signs, buses pulled up whenever the driver spotted potential customers.

The old lady waving an umbrella on the pavement would bring the bus right up to the kerb and the conductor would dexterously lift her aboard with an almost affectionate hug.

Speed was of the essence.

*The daily earnings of each conveyance depend so much on the joint efforts of driver and conductor that they do not scruple to urge on their steeds when it suits their convenience. The demands thus made upon the strength of the horses soon renders them unfit for the road. I have been assured ... that such horses as are employed will, on an average, stand omnibus work no longer than eight years.*

The largest buses, drawn by three horses, were those connecting to railway stations. Seating was divided into first and second class. One route led from Piccadilly Circus to Charing Cross, another from the Circus to Baker Street.

The decline of the horse bus began at the turn of the century when the first motor buses were plying for hire. By 1913 there were 3,000 motor buses in London. Congested streets, not least Piccadilly, led to heated arguments between drivers and loud protests from passengers.

*Where a choice was offered, it was the younger people who boarded the motor bus, the more mature stuck to the horse bus. They watched each other stealthily – at least the 'outside' passengers did – as they went along, sometimes side by side. The motor bus would do its best to pass the horse bus and frequently succeeded.*

While the horse was king, the hansom cab was the smart way of getting about.

*Mr Hansom, the inventor, designed a vehicle that was unique. It was a light, swift, comfortable – yes, and handsome – and I don't think such a perfectly satisfactory metropolitan carriage had ever been seen before or is likely to be seen again. No modern carriage can give the occupants such a sense of languid opulence or provide such a suitable setting for a real swell. It was the ideal décor for an opera hat and a white tie; the most callow youth thus dressed and mounted looked truly regal.*

The hansom had two large wheels. It carried just two passengers and was driven by a cabman seated behind the passengers.

*The driver always looked a picture perched high upon his back seat. His broad seamed boxcloth coat was usually adorned with large pearlies, and he generally wore the first, or artificial last, rose of summer in his buttonhole, and a squat top-hat, tilted jauntily, which shone like the finest black lacquer through having been treated with a prepara-*

*tion of which Guinness's stout was the chief ingredient. All this completed a decidedly gay and sporting makeup.*

The four-wheeler or 'growlers' were the poor relation of the hansom, driven for the most part by 'extremely old men who endeavoured to look as ancient as their horses'.

The early motor cars, mostly French imports, added to traffic noise and confusion. A rich man's toy, they were seen as a status symbol, one that was enhanced by having a French chauffeur – he was always the chauffeur, never the driver.

# 11
# His Hour upon the Stage

Writing his Theatrical Notes in 1893, Joseph Knight declared: 'That the stage is in a more flourishing condition now than any time in the last half century, few would deny.'

With six new theatres in Shaftesbury Avenue alone and the rise to celebrity of the acting profession, there were fortunes to be made.

The proximity to theatreland made Piccadilly and Albany, in particular, an attractive home for actors, writers and others linked to the drama. Two of the unforgettable personalities were Squire (originally Sidney) Bancroft and Herbert Beerbohm Tree, both actor managers who had their own theatres, chose the plays to be presented, acted and directed and kept control of the box office. A flamboyant glamour attached to their names.

In the 1880s, when Bancroft and Tree were making their names, the undisputed head of the profession was Henry Irving who, with his leading lady, Ellen Terry, ruled over the Lyceum Theatre in Wellington Street, just off the Strand. But Irving's melodramatic style was going out of fashion when Bancroft, with his wife, Marie, 'the little Victorian pigeon', presented a succession of light 'drawing room' comedies which made no pretence at being anything but a happy diversion from the daily grind.

Actor manager, Sir Squire Bancroft, by H G
Riviere, courtesy of the Garrick Club, London

In 1879, Bancroft took on the lease of the Haymarket Theatre where they rebuilt the interior to make a comfortable and attractive auditorium. The cheap seats in the pit made way for the orchestra, partially hidden by the stage. Low price tickets were restricted to the gallery. Among their other innovations was the matinée, soon to be *de rigueur* for every theatre. Actors engaged by the Bancrofts were decently treated with dressing rooms that allowed for more than swinging a cat and generous wages.

Having made their money, the Bancrofts entered on a long and happy retirement. Knighted in 1897, two years after Irving, Sir Squire was often to be seen in one of the windows of his Albany chambers feeding his pet canary 'Carousa'. His monocle, cascading white hair, top hat and cane were a familiar sight at first nights and at more sombre events. According to the caricaturist, Harry Furness, 'There is hardly ever a memorial service for any well-known person that Sir Squire does not attend [and] he is familiar with every obituary notice.

After the departure of the Bancrofts, the Haymarket was taken over by Herbert Beerbohm Tree who also had an Albany apartment. Tree brought magic to the theatre. It was not just his ability to mould his personality to the demands of any role but his talent for creating scenes that catapulted the audience into the action. Here is Tree's biographer, Hesketh Pearson, on giving the edge to Shakespeare.

*Just before his entrance in Macbeth there was a long roll of thunder, a roar of wind and a rattle of hail; the darkness was suddenly pierced by blinding flashes of lightning, in which one could see rocks falling and a stout oak-tree, rent to the roots, toppling to the earth; following this the elements howled invisibly for a space; then came an ear-*

*splitting peal of thunder, a final shriek of the blast, and
against the dazzling background of lightning-riven sky
stood the figure of Macbeth. Then Shakespeare got a look-
in. Emerging from the theatre after one of these stage-quak-
ing exhibitions into a real thunderstorm, one had to admit
that Nature put up a pretty feeble imitation of what several
barrels of stones and a few sheets of tin could do.*

Tree varied his performances to suit his mood, no two evenings were
the same. This was anathema to Irving who, having established a role,
never departed from his first interpretation. Of the many Irving jibes
at his rival, the best was thought too *risqué* for polite Victorian society. It happened when Irving was inspecting a horse that was needed
to carry him on stage. Seeking to reassure him, the owner vouched
for the animal's even temper, adding that it had carried Beerbohm
Tree without ever causing concern. At this point the horse broke
wind, very loudly. 'Ah,' said Irving, 'a bit of a critic too, eh?'

Artistic and financial success at the Haymarket encouraged Tree in his ambition to build his own theatre. Opposite the
Haymarket was the ideal site, formerly the home of the Opera
House. Devastated by fire in 1867, it was eight years before a new
Opera House was opened and by then it had lost its appeal and its
standing as one of London's three leading theatres. A scheme for a
new theatre and a hotel being finally agreed, Beerbohm Tree came
into his own. Designed by Charles J. Phipps, a leading theatre architect, Her Majesty's (renamed His Majesty's after the accession
of Edward VII) opened in 1897, the year of Phipps's death. 'It rises
spaciously and brilliantly to the dignity of art,' wrote Bernard Shaw.

The first production was Shakespeare's *Julius Caesar* with scenery and costumes by Lawrence Alma-Tadema. With Tree playing Antony, critical acclaim gave it the accolade of the best Shakespearian production in living memory. The play ran for five months and made a thumping profit.

Tree built on his reputation for giving audiences more than they bargained for:

> *In the opening scene of The Tempest a ship rocked on a realistic sea, the waves splashed and the wind roared; in Antony and Cleopatra the text had to be re-arranged to suit the scenery, the return of Antony to Alexandria, which is the occasion of one speech in the text, being illustrated by a tableau in which excited crowds and dancing girls were a prelude to the arrival to music, first of Cleopatra, then of Antony. In Richard II real horses were introduced in the Lists at Coventry, and Tree as Richard entered London on a horse in place of the speech in which the Duke of York merely describes this happening.*

It was the Bancrofts' contention that a manager had to have the courage to withdraw a play while it was still paying instead of letting it die a slow death. It would then be available for revival when the time was right. Tree might have added that boredom was a good reason as any for cutting short a successful run. This is what happened with the premiere of Shaw's *Pygmalion* with Tree as Professor Higgins. Fearing what liberties Tree would make of his play, Shaw refused to put in an appearance at the theatre until the hundredth performance. He then discovered to his horror that

Tree had inserted a happy ending by throwing a bunch of flowers to Eliza in the few seconds between the end of the play and the fall of the curtain. Shaw protested.

'My ending makes money; you ought to be grateful,' said Tree. 'Your ending is damnable; you ought to be shot,' Shaw replied.

Though George Alexander did not live in Piccadilly (his blue plaque tells us that his home was in Pont Street, Chelsea) he, more than any other actor manager, embodied the spirit of the place. It was not just that his theatre, the St James's, was in King Street adjacent to Piccadilly but also that Alexander himself lived up to the popular image of the Piccadilly gentleman – debonair with perfect manners, never excited or rushed, a model of effortless charm.

Serving his apprenticeship with Irving at the Lyceum, the great man took Alexander to task over his interpretation of Macduff, the victim of Macbeth's savagery. 'Macduff, you know – a man of violent rage, a man of blood and steel – hardly anything of Piccadilly.'

Like Bancroft, Alexander was a shrewd administrator who gave theatregoers creature comforts with the installation of plush seats and electric light. But his true skill was as a talent spotter. His first success was *Lady Windermere's Fan*. So confident was he of Oscar Wilde's ability to deliver that he paid him a £100 advance on royalties before even a line or even a scenario had been written. Having read the finished play, he offered to buy it outright for £1,000. The canny Wilde responded, 'I have so much confidence in your excellent judgement, my dear Aleck, that I cannot but refuse your generous offer.' It was a wise decision. Wilde made £7,000 from the play's run at the St James's. In May 1893, Alexander presented *The Second Mrs Tanqueray* by Arthur W. Pinero. Noting the growing influence of Ibsen, with his social dramas, Pinero aimed at a 'rational, observant, home-grown play'. His theme, by Victorian standards, was controversial. What were middle class audiences to make of the tragic consequences of a marriage between a middle-aged widower and a woman with a past? As Alexander's co-star, Mrs Patrick Campbell marvelled at London's youngest actor-manager being able to get the play past the Censor.

In her first big role, the mercurial Mrs Pat triumphed over a recent bout of typhoid fever to give the play the emotional power it needed to break through the barrier of social convention. As the curtain fell, the *Daily News* reported how,

> *... pent-up emotions found relief in a storm of applause which did not subside until the leading players had appeared again and again and the author had responded to a call which shook the walls of the theatre.*

The *Evening Standard* heralded 'a great play', a verdict repeated in *The Echo*, which continued 'and a great actress'. But the 'great actress' was temperamental. 'She became notorious for the havoc she caused ... through a mixture of caprice and moodiness, a liking for practical joking and a sharp tongue.'

A year later, Wilde sent Alexander his 'somewhat farcical comedy', *The Importance of Being Earnest*. Despite constant interference by Wilde, doubtless made nervous by the threat of legal proceedings against him, Alexander produced a palpable hit, albeit a short one. With Wilde's arrest, the box office dwindled and the play had to be taken off.

By the turn of the century, Alexander was tiring of acting and producing. While he was still relatively young, he turned his mind to politics and was elected to the London County Council. But he had left it too late for a second career. In 1911, when he was knighted, diabetes and tuberculosis were draining him of energy. He died in 1918.

Dion Boucicault was well past his best when, in 1883, he took up residency at Albany. But what an extraordinary career he had to look back on. Writer, actor and impresario, the Irish-born Boucicault was hardly out of his teens when he wrote *London Assurance*, one of the few original plays of the period thought worthy of revival. He was a chancer, his life marked out by giddily high achievements followed by collapse. Fortunes came and went. In 1845, he married a wealthy French widow who fell off a cliff while on a walking tour of Switzerland. Her death was never adequately explained. Boucicault was a widower at age twenty-seven.

Success came with his clever use of special effects of his 'sensation plays'. In *The Colleen Bawn* ('fair girl') he fabricated a rescue on a moonlit lake. Audiences were wholly convinced by a stage covering of gauze to suggest a watery grave while failing to notice the trap-door through which the fair girl sank before resurfacing.

Boucicault played the stock character of an Irish 'broth of a boy' but so convincingly as to overcome all critical reservations. *The Colleen Bawn* was the first play to achieve a long run on the modern scale, lasting through the severe winter of 1860/61 when many London theatres were forced to close.

Riding high on the triumph of *The Colleen Bawn*, Boucicault struck a blow for all dramatists by demanding a royalty of half of net profits on box office takings, a radical departure from the modest straight fee usually offered to playwrights. With the dramatists' art taken more seriously by managers and by audiences, Boucicault may be said to be one of the leading founders of modern theatre.

Boucicault kept up his output of sensationalist plays, with the most famous of all sensation scenes mounted for *After Dark*, which featured the rescue of a man lying helpless on a railway line at the mercy of an oncoming train. The plot device became a cliché of early movies.

Boucicault did not have long to enjoy his Albany apartment. Ever restless, no sooner had he settled in than he embarked on a tour of Australia. Whilst there he married a young actress before his divorce from his current wife had been finalised. The scandal of 'bigamy with adultery' added real spice to a career built on stage melodrama. After a series of heart attacks, Boucicault died in New York in 1890.

Three months before the outbreak of the Great War, the New York born playwright and novelist, Edward Knoblock, took rooms in Albany. Best known for his 1911 play *Kismet*, later a successful musical, Knoblock was a rather dour character. He nonetheless favoured a wildly exotic interior design for his Albany apartment.

Arnold Bennett, who borrowed the flat during Knoblock's absence in Paris, gave a description in his novel *Pretty Lady*. The furnishing, he wrote, was in the colourful Regency style inspired by the Royal Pavilion in Brighton.

> *His dome bed was yellow as to its upper works, with crimson valances above and yellow valances below. The yellow-*

*lined crimson curtains (of course, never closed) had green
cords and tassels, and the counterpane was yellow. The bed
was a modest sample of the careful and uncompromising
reconstitution of a period which he had everywhere carried
out in his abode.*

Knoblock himself went into more detail. 'The principal room
(with a huge eighteenth century bow-window and balcony facing Vigo Street) was very large and exceptionally lofty – about
twenty feet high. I am not exaggerating, for adjacent to it were
two small rooms one above the other, the upper being reached by
a tiny winding staircase. The one below I made my bedroom – the
one above a very small dining-room.

'Leading off the big room was another smaller room connected with an archway. Here I had my books and did my writing.
In the big room was a piano, a huge sofa in the bow-window, a
Récamier couch and various cabinets – all, of course, of solemn
Regency. The walls were marbled in a deep sienna and varnished,
softly reflecting the light from the window at day-time, and the
candle-light at night. As a border for the various panels into
which the walls were cut up I found an old model in the hall of
a Club, which had not been altered for a hundred years. It was a
variation of the Greek key-pattern, very beautiful and intricate. I
engaged a special artist to do this painting, which took him over
two months to complete.'

His curtains, a deep purple with a palm leaf border of bronze,
he had woven specially for him at Lyons.

Knoblock was in Albany in 1917 when there were Zeppelin raids on central London. Late one afternoon he was visited by the husband and wife artists, John and Hazel Lavery, the latter a stunning beauty and socialite for whom the war was a minor inconvenience, not to be taken too seriously. Announcing their arrival she told Knoblock, 'We were just helping to arrange a small Rembrandt Exhibition at the Burlington Fine Arts Club, when we heard the siren. So we took all the pictures into the cellar. And now we've come and would like to stay here, as we have a dinner at the Ritz. And we don't want to go all the way home [to Kennington]. Do you mind?'

Knoblcok was only too delighted.

*We sat and talked and Hazel was telling me of a string of pearls that John had promised her for Christmas. By this time the bombs of the aeroplanes had begun to fall. But this didn't put Hazel off in the least – so thrilled was she at the prospect of the promised present.*

*'Now would you have large pearls of a less fine quality?' she asked me, 'or – ' and she stopped as a bomb crashed. 'Listen! There's another one –' she added casually and then continued. 'Or would you have a string of smaller pearls of – ' She stopped again. 'There's another bomb closer,' she interrupted herself. 'Or smaller pearls of the best quality – There! That one nearly got us, didn't it? Now John says that big pearls are more becoming to me!' – Bang – Bang – 'But I think –'*

*And so she went on chatting gaily till I finally suggested*
*our going down into the cellar. We did so, my good servant*
*carrying an electric torch to light the way.*

Though this anecdote belies Knoblock's reputation as a dull companion, a counter story was told of Sir John Gielgud, famous for his *faux pas*.

Lunching with Gielgud at the Garrick Club, Knoblock caught him waving to someone across the room. 'Who's that?' he asked. Gielgud said airily, 'The second most boring man in London.' 'Who's first?' asked Knoblock. Gielgud responded, 'Without doubt, Edward Knoblock.' Then realising what he had said, 'But not you, my dear fellow. The other Edward Knoblock.'

Of greater impact on popular entertainment than all the Albany theatrical worthies put together was Fred Karno who took up residence in 1917 after the breakup of his marriage. The master of slapstick comedy who gave the music hall its distinctive flavour, Karno, though little remembered now, can take credit for launching the careers of Charlie Chaplin and Stan Laurel. In the Great War, the self-deprecating humour of the troops gave us:

*We are Fred Karno's Army*
*Fred Karno's infantry*
*We cannot fight, we cannot shoot*
*So what damn good are we?*

Sung to the tune of the hymn 'The Church's One Foundation'.

# 12

# By Popular Demand

By the 1890s, a shopping revolution was underway. Retailers extended their reach beyond the big spenders living close by to cater for the middle class visitors to the West End who demanded style at affordable prices. This required large ground floor window displays and open interiors which in turn called for the rebuilding of premises no longer fit for purpose.

An early indication of what was in prospect came with redevelopment of the St James's Hall and restaurant complex between Piccadilly and Regent Street. The loss of the Hall was thought to be of no great consequence, its function as a concert venue having been taken over by the superior Queen's Hall in Langham Place. But the reconstruction of such a large site raised questions as to the future of the Circus end of Piccadilly. Seeking a uniform design, a government appointed committee of three leading architects recommended that the problem should be handed over to Richard Norman Shaw, an architect famous for New Scotland

Yard on the Victoria Embankment (now called the Norman Shaw Buildings) and for setting the style of Bedford Park in Chiswick, the first garden suburb.

The lights go up on Piccadilly

When he accepted the commission to reconfigure the Quadrant and Piccadilly Circus, then still known as Regent Circus South, Shaw was aged seventy-three and no longer active professionally. But the scale of the challenge appealed to his love of the grand plan. In a burst of creative energy, he produced a new layout for Piccadilly Circus allowing for a much-needed widening of the connecting roads.

The scheme foundered on the absence of cooperation between public bodies, the government's refusal to give financial backing and the opposition of retailers who complained of Shaw's failure to provide adequate window space.

However, a revised plan for the Piccadilly Hotel to be built on the site of St James's Hall was approved. This incorporated, on the Piccadilly side, a deep recess with gabled wings joined by a columned screen running the length of the building. At best, an identifying feature it had limited use and was judged by many to be a waste of space. For some odd reason, the break in the façade allowed for building higher than would otherwise have been permitted. The hotel opened in 1908 and is now called the Dilly.

With his main proposals rejected and with no further rebuilding in prospect, Shaw decided to call it a day. But there was one positive result from his efforts. The completion of Shaftesbury Avenue, albeit too narrow, and the demolition of most of Swallow Street allowed for a Piccadilly Circus three times bigger than the original.

Leading the campaign to make Piccadilly more attractive to shoppers was the department store Swan & Edgar which in its heyday claimed to cater for 'every need for men, women and children' with 'all articles of fashion of the latest styles and reliable quality'.

George Swan, a Ludgate draper, opened for business at No. 20 Piccadilly in 1814. When his shop was lost to the expansion of the Circus, he moved to the corner between Piccadilly and Regent Street. Having taken his young assistant, William Edgar, into partnership, the shop continued to thrive. Edgar became sole proprietor after Swan's death in 1821. The firm passed out of family hands in 1886 but by then Swan & Edgar was one of the foremost department stores, serving customers, said managing director Walter Morford, who were 'too elegant to have their clothes made locally yet not sufficiently acquainted with London to discover good dressmaking within their means'.

In 1896 the *Fortnightly Review* waxed lyrical on the allure of Swan & Edgar where 'there are so many things we never thought of buying until they presented their fascination on every side'. Adding to the temptation to spend were the female assistants who 'are so much quicker than men in understanding what other women want'.

A Swan & Edgar sales catalogue of the time is equally seductive though some items might have warranted a health warning. The 'finest corset' was 'constructed with numerous curved pieces of quality whalebone and steel (to ensure that) the abdominal flesh is pressed flat'.

Swan & Edgar had two rebirths. Having opposed Norman Shaw's designs (Walter Morford dismissed them as 'utterly absurd for commercial purposes') the store had better luck with Shaw's successor, Sir Reginald Blomfield who succeeded in rebuilding Nash's County Fire Office, an insurance headquarters now part of the Hotel Café Royal, and in giving Swan & Edgar a long shallow curve on the corner of Piccadilly and Regent Street. Rebuilt yet again in 1924-27, to allow for a higher elevation, the old Swan & Edgar, though no longer a department store, is still a dominant feature of the Circus.

Another distinguished retailer at the Circus end of Piccadilly is Cordings at No19, still holding to its original brief of selling sturdy rainwear. Setting up as an outfitter in 1839 in the Strand, John Charles Cording moved his shop to Piccadilly in 1877. The

Cordings speciality was, and remains, waterproof coats and boots, essential for country wear and, in the early days of the motoring, for drivers of open top cars. The basement at No19 was for many years the Cordings workshop.

After the family sold out in 1971 there were hard times until Eric Clapton, world famous guitarist and songwriter, joined a management buyout. Now established as the home of country clothing, Cordings has extended its range to cater for a growing roster of women customers.

One of the first buildings to occupy the enlarged Piccadilly Circus was the London Pavilion, a music hall to match the grandeur of the news theatres in Shaftesbury Avenue. Still recognisable by its façade, though now a shopping arcade, part of the Trocadero Centre, the Pavilion had a shady beginning. The site on which once stood the Black Horse Inn, was bought by the Metropolitan Board of Works in 1879. It was then leased to R E Villiers, a property developer of dubious reputation. By bribing public officials, Villiers was granted an artificially low ground rent. When the Pavilion eventually opened it was not so much a place of entertainment as a drinking den and the haunt of sex workers. It was only after Villiers sold out at a handsome profit, that an upmarket Pavilion was created.

Praising the cream and gold interior, *The Era* noted that 'all the floors are fitted with elegantly appointed lavatories', a luxury then and it might be added by the modern theatre goers, a rare luxury still.

It was the impresario, Charles B. Cochran who gave the Pavilion its glory days. His association began in 1918 after a successful management of the circus at Olympia. His formula for the Pavilion centred on revues in which prominence was given to 'Mr Cochran's Young Ladies', a chorus line of unrivalled charm and beauty. Front of house publicity always gave the star billing to Cochran who, after all, was the presiding genius of a string of money spinning productions.

The reshaping of Piccadilly Circus had its effect on Leicester Square. Up to the time of Charles II, the Square was a rustic backwater where the family home of the Leicesters was the dominant building. Decline set in with the breakup of the Leicester estates and the demolition of Leicester House in 1791.

Various attempts to generate public entertainments included Wyld's Great Globe with its giant scale map of the world and the Panopticon, a Moorish palace built on the east side of the square in 1854 for displays 'to assist by moral and intellectual agencies the best interests of society'. When, like the Great Globe, it failed at the box office, a new owner had better luck with a licence for music, dancing, drinking and smoking. So was born the Alhambra, a performance space that introduced the public to the Amazing Leotard, the 'daring young man on the flying trapeze' and to Sarah Wright, better known as 'The Kicker' whose long legs and short skirts made her the foremost practitioner of the Can-can, the latest craze from Paris. While ineffable Sarah was the toast of the London clubs, the licensing authority took a less sanguine view. Sarah departed to Islington where Collins' Music Hall was only too happy to put her at the top of the bill.

After a fire all but destroyed the Alhambra, the opportunity was taken to start anew with a state of the art music hall, one of

London's largest. When it opened, Leicester Square had a new face. For decades, the open space at the centre had served as a garbage dump. It was transformed from a 'filthy wilderness into a blooming garden' by Albert Grant, a Tory politician who bought the site, planted trees, laid out flower beds and put up a statue to Shakespeare copied from the Bard's memorial in Westminster Abbey. The glowing dedication to Grant on the pedestal fails to mention that Leicester Square's benefactor was also a financial rogue. Caught out on his promotion of fictitious companies, Grant appeared twice in the bankruptcy court before descending into penury.

By the time of his departure, the Alhambra shared Leicester Square with a popular rival. The Empire was the same but different. While the Alhambra was the meeting place for men of all ranks out for a good time, the Empire was more of an annexe to London's smartest clubs.

*The Empire Lounge was known throughout Britain and her Dominions as a place where soldiers and sailors back from foreign service, or travellers who had not been in England for many a year, could make almost certain of meeting someone with whom they had been acquainted in the old days, and in this they were seldom disappointed. It was here that old friendships were renewed and long-forgotten comrades contacted, so it is not to be wondered at that many a wanderer found his way to the Empire purely in search of a perfectly virtuous evening.*

The respectability was wafer thin. As popular as any entertainment on stage were the promenades where ladies of easy virtue paraded their talents. Such blatant soliciting raised the ire of the League of Purity led by Mrs Ormiston Chant, a doughty campaigner who fought vigorously for the closure of both theatres.

Cheered on by a small army of vigilantes or 'prudes on patrol', as the *Daily Telegraph* called them, Mrs Chant succeeded in having the Empire's promenades shut down and for a ban on the sale of alcohol in the auditorium. To get back into a profitable business, the management put up a partition to separate audiences from those who were simply out for a good time. This did not go down well with the young regulars who made their protest by pulling down the offending barricade. Among their number was a 21-year-old Sandhurst cadet, Winston Churchill.

Despite the best efforts of the high-minded, the music hall became embedded in British culture. Piccadilly was a great source of material for singers and comedy turns. Fun was to be had at the expense of the Crutch and Toothpick Brigade, a brotherhood of young men who haunted the promenades and stage doors, each sporting a black silver-mounted crutch stick and a toothpick held languidly between the teeth.

Piccadilly fashions were an ever-flowing source of music-hall jokes. Piccadilly weepers were long, carefully combed side whiskers; a monocle was called a Piccadilly window; while a Piccadilly fringe was a female hairstyle with the hair cut short and curled back over the forehead. There was even a loping walk known as the Piccadilly crawl.

A recurring character on stage, often seen for real in Piccadilly, was the model of shabby gentility, conveying pride and independence in ragged but clean attire. These gentlemen of the streets were famously portrayed as Burlington Berties, first performed in 1900 by Vesta Tilly but more memorably in a later version by Ella Shields who sang of Burlington Bertie from Bow.

*I'm Burlington Bertie I rise at ten-thirty and saunter along like a toff*

*I walk down the Strand with my gloves in my hand*

*Then walk down again with them off.*

If, despite the Burlington reference, Bertie must be counted more of the Strand than Piccadilly, there was no question of the location for Silk Hat Tony who told his audience that he was down and out, broken and bent. But he held fast to the belief that Piccadilly had been built especially for him.

*I said to the King once at tea*
*They built you a Palace*
*I bear you no malice*
*They built Piccadilly for me ...*

As the leading male impersonator Hetty King sang of Piccadilly 'the playground of the gay where the traffic goes one way', warning, with a broad wink, that at night time 'you're apt to lose your wife'.

As the identifying symbol of London, rivalled only by Big Ben and Tower Bridge, Eros was unveiled in 1893. The world famous winged cherub atop his plinth in Piccadilly Circus was originally intended to depict Anteros, the Greek god of selfless love; this as a tribute to Lord Shaftesbury, the Victorian philanthropist and campaigner against child labour. The popular restyling of the sculpture as Eros, god of sensuality, could not have been more inappropriate since Shaftesbury, who spent lavishly on schemes for social regeneration was also a moral campaigner who advocated a blanket prohibition on anything that might 'sanction the representation of sin'. What would he have made of a naked youth, delicately poised on one leg, firing his arrow of desire into the crowd?

The making of Eros was not a happy experience for his sculptor. In the forefront of his profession, Alfred Gilbert, judged by many to be on a par with Rodin, favoured a more vital and lifelike representation of his subjects in contrast to the formulaic statues of political and military worthies occupying many a town square.

In choosing to work in aluminium, then a rare metal, Gilbert incurred expense that was way beyond his budget. To add to his troubles, the bronze memorial fountain, a pulpit-like basin that provided a pedestal for Eros, proved controversial. Intended as a drinking fountain, no sooner was it in service than the cups provided for free refreshment were broken off their chains and carried off as souvenirs. If Eros did not make the grade in quite the way expected of him, he soon became a favourite with the public. Flower sellers, with their loaded baskets, made their market place on the steps to the fountain. 'Buy a flower for a pretty lady' was the cry heard by every young couple on their night out.

It was thanks to Eros that Piccadilly Circus became the first choice for national celebrations though what precisely was being celebrated and why was not always clear. For forty years or more, the wildest Piccadilly party followed the Oxford and Cambridge Boat Race. Few of the revellers had any direct association with the two universities though most felt at home with gentlemanly sports. Togged up in formal evening gear, young bucks were intent on having a ball. They shouted, they danced, they did all sorts of things. Queer, improvised round dances grew and grew until hundreds were capering. Young men felt impelled to ride on the roof of hansom cabs and shout all the while.

Out in force, the police were inclined to indulge high spirits while drawing the line at attempts to acquire a 'bobby's' helmet as a souvenir. The likely consequence was a night in the cells followed by an appearance before a sour-faced magistrate. P.G. Wodehouse made this a running joke in his Bertie Wooster stories.

A genuinely national celebration, albeit of dubious credentials, took possession of Piccadilly for five days in May 1900. This 'orgy of patriotic emotion' that has never been equalled – surpassing Armistice Day, 1918 and VE Day, 1945 – was sparked by news of the relief of Mafeking 'a tiny settlement of tin-roofed houses, at the edge of the Kalahari Desert in South Africa, a place virtually unheard of seven months before.'

The background was a colonial war which had proved an embarrassment to Britain. In South Africa there were two British colonies, the Cape and Natal; and two Boer (Dutch) republics, the Orange Free State and the Transvaal. When the struggle for ascendancy descended into war, an ill-prepared British army found itself outwitted and outmatched by a dedicated force of guerrilla fighters. The job of Colonel Robert Baden-Powell of the

13th Hussars was to patrol the frontier with Transvaal. But for reason best known to himself, he took half the men 200 miles south to Mafeking, a town of no strategic importance where he prepared for a siege that he alone was predicting.

With his talent for self-promotion, Baden-Powell encouraged war reporters to spice up their dispatches with romanticised stories of British pluck. Yet sporadic raids and an artillery bombardment caused little damage. *The Times* correspondent recorded a 'farcical melodrama'. Even so, when, eventually, Mafeking was liberated, as it was bound to be once the British army got its act together, there was a collective sigh of relief. The Empire had escaped the ignominy of defeat by a ragtag and bobtail militia.

Overnight, Baden-Powell became Britain's favourite soldier. That he was not awarded high military honours suggests that his superiors kept a sense of proportion. Everybody else went wild.

*The news broke quite late in the evening. It was announced in the theatres, restaurants and music halls. The West End converged on Piccadilly Circus. Such scenes will never come again. ... To say pandemonium broke loose is to understate. All reserve vanished like a theatre curtain ascending, people embraced, everybody seemed to be old friends bent on celebrating. They sang, they danced, they made high holiday. Street vendors appeared as if by magic, everybody had a Union Jack, everybody had a tickler and many had squirts. To the uninitiated a tickler was a peacock feather, peddled at one penny, with which you tickled everybody within reach. A squirt spoke for itself.*

High on celebrity, the feted hero went on to found a world-wide youth movement.

Unless they lived nearby, the celebrants of Mafeking had to make their way to Piccadilly on foot or by public transport on streets that were clogged long before they reached their destination. This all changed in 1906 when the underground railway came to Piccadilly. So popular was it that passenger numbers increased from 1·5 million in 1907 to 18 million in 1922. By then, the station was in urgent need of enlargement.

The problem was in finding the space to expand. The challenge was taken up by Frank Pick, the commercial manager of London Underground, whose understanding of commercial design and what it could achieve amounted to genius. At his right hand was architect Charles Holden who had designed many of the new stations on the Piccadilly line.

Since it was out of the question to dominate the Circus with a new building, the only feasible solution was to dig down to create a subterranean booking hall. The excavation was hideously complicated. Piccadilly was at the hub of a network of pipes and cables that fed central London with essential services. But there were no records to show what was actually under the Circus. Trenches dug across roads feeding into the Circus revealed a labyrinth of telegraph cables, telephone lines, Post Office pneumatic tubes, water pipes, hydraulic mains and sewers. Before construction could begin, all these tributaries had to be redirected into a twelve-foot tunnel. Eros was moved to the Embankment Gardens. He was absent from Piccadilly for nine years.

As a spur to public interest, a full-scale model of the oval booking hall went on display at Earl's Court. An eagerly anticipated innovation was the installation of automatic ticket dispensers to cut down on queues at the ticket office. Escalators, still a novelty, promised relief for the foot weary. With a generous allowance of space to move about, the booking hall was a favourite for commercial exhibitions. One of the companies to take early advantage of a captive audience was Frigidaire with a demonstration of products deemed essential for the modern kitchen.

When the new Piccadilly tube station opened in 1928, the scale of its ambitions was illustrated by a five panel mural above the escalators. The work of Stephen Bone, now best known as a war artist, it depicted the delights on offer to the tube traveller including theatre and shopping excursions and weekend breaks in the countryside. For the central mural, a map of the world had London at the centre with Piccadilly at the heart of the Empire. There was some truth in this. Piccadilly was open to the world.

*For from all corners of the earth they come, all races, creeds and colours, to visit Piccadilly Circus. They gaze and they wonder. Men and women, youths and girls, in all sorts of attire sit around the base of Eros, and watch the traffic revolve, feeling the world go round. They are supremely happy. They stay there for hours. I have asked them why they do it and it is always the same reply. 'This is the centre of all things, you know. We can hear the heart of the world throb.' The phraseology is different but the sentiment is the same, and it comes in all languages. ... This place is magic.*

Over the top? A little perhaps though certain it is that by the 1930s, the public had adopted Piccadilly Circus as its own. Londoners who had generally kept to their home patch now gravitated to the Circus for a day 'up West'.

The lights were an added attraction, much to the distress of the authorities. As early as 1900, the London County Council proposed a ban on all illuminated advertisements, arguing that flashing lights were a distraction for drivers. But the necessary approval by the Home Office was limited to a ban only when there was a 'clear danger to traffic', a proviso that was almost impossible to prove. Advertisers felt free to occupy the frontage of buildings where Shaftesbury Avenue opened into Piccadilly Circus. In 1908 an illuminated invitation to Drink Perrier Water was erected on the parapet over the entrance to the Café Monico. Two years later, it was joined by Bovril and Schweppes while a baby with an illuminated forelock was seen sucking a bottle of Nestlé's milk. With the LCC powerless to intervene, *The Times* came out with an attack on a 'hideous eyesore which no civilized community ought to tolerate'. But by then the Piccadilly lights were a popular fixture that even had its appeal to the aristocracy, if only for certain financial benefits.

In the 1920s the advertising agency, J. Walter Thompson, had the bright idea of recruiting young attractive, titled ladies to glamorise their images. One of these was Lady Marguerite Strickland who, despite being a teetotaller, promoted Gordon's Gin. Her appearance on an illuminated hoarding on Piccadilly Circus was to proclaim the therapeutic qualities of Horlicks.

*There was a picture of me about thirty feet high, with a spotlight on it. And it had written across it, 'Do You Suffer From Night Starvation?' One evening Jimmy Horlick and my father were going past in a taxi and Jimmy Horlick, not knowing who the picture was of, because my name wasn't on it, asked: 'Have you seen my advertisement up there?' My father replied, 'Yes, that's my daughter.'*

# 13
# Albany under Threat

By the end of the century, Albany was losing its shine as London's smartest bachelor address. Ill-equipped apartments opening on to draughty stone staircases did not meet the standards of modern living. Dry rot, leaking roofs and bulging walls failed to pass the most cursory survey. In 1893, fifteen sets were unoccupied and were likely to remain so until the plumbing had been renewed and electricity installed. The mood of defeatism was exacerbated by the competition from purpose-built mansion flats offering all the latest conveniences. There was talk of winding up the Trust and calling in the estate agents.

Then along galloped a white knight. William Stone was thirty-six when he moved into Albany in 1893. A single man of more than adequate means and time on his hands, he was soon elected a trustee. Shortly afterwards, he was made chairman, continuing in office until well into old age.

The interests and prestige of Albany became his life's preoc-cupation. Setting in train an ambitious refurbishment, he backed his judgement by investing in the property. When he died in 1958, shortly after completing his century, he owned eleven sets of rooms.

The source of Stone's wealth remains a mystery. While a fam-ily inheritance came his way, it did not cover a lifestyle that put him into a higher income bracket. In addition to his investment in Albany, it allowed for a Mayfair mansion in Curzon Street.

The likeliest explanation for Stone's apparently effortless promotion to a man of property was his friendship with Cecil Rhodes 'who struck me as a most amiable man ... [one who] gave me some good financial advice'. Doubtless this was linked to the gold and diamond mining boom in South Africa.

After graduating first class in natural sciences at Peterhouse College, Cambridge, in 1878, he set off on his travels first to Egypt and then to India and South Africa where he made his reputa-tion as a big game hunter. Returning to London, he furnished his Albany apartment with hunting trophies including elephants' feet, tiger skins and stuffed pythons, cobras, lizards and crocodiles. *The Sportsman* featured him as one of the 'Celebrities with the Gun'.

Short and dapper with a waxed moustache, he was always the natty dresser, sporting a carnation button hole when out riding in the morning which he changed to a gardenia after lunch. He lived frugally, a modest eater and drinker who never smoked. While we might guess that he could bore with stories of his confrontations with wild beasts, he enjoyed company and was a member of some dozen clubs.

Stone never missed the chance to raise the profile of Albany. One of his early conquests was John Lane, joint founder of the publisher Bodley Head based at 6B Vigo Street, opposite the rear entrance to Albany. Lane was a shrewd businessman who could see a bright future for book publishing. With the expansion of literacy and the removal of taxes on knowledge, it was a boom time for literature. Steam power had revolutionised printing while cheap wood-pulp paper and new paper-making machines had brought down the cost of producing books and journals.

When Lane and William Stone first got together, Lane had made his name and risked his reputation as the publisher of *The Yellow Book*, an illustrated quarterly aimed to be both journal and a book, at once topical but of such high production values as to justify a place on library shelves.

As to content, *The Yellow Book* set out to push against the boundaries of literature while stopping short of incensing arbiters of public taste. Said the editor, 'while *The Yellow Book* will seek always to preserve a delicate, decorous, and reticent mien and conduct, it will at the same time have the courage of its modernness, and not tremble at the frown of Mrs Grundy.' The pledge was easier to state than to implement. While a roster of established writers underscored convention, the appointment of Aubrey Beardsley as art director was controversial. At twenty-one, Beardsley was already famous for his illustrations for the English edition of Oscar Wilde's *Salome*. Advertised, much to Wilde's distress as 'the play the Lord Chamberlain refused to license', Beardsley's striking images of androgynous figures, standing apart from any relationship to the play, shocked John Lane as publisher as much as they upset the author. Both demanded a toning down, Beardsley was undeterred. In the late stages of tuberculosis, he knew that time was short. He made it known that as art director of *The Yellow Book*, he was not averse to content that was 'perhaps a little *risqué*'.

The first edition, appearing in April 1894, revealed what Beardsley had in mind. The cover was of a leering masked woman who could not be other than a prostitute. Inside, the book was another provocative picture, this of an aging whore instructing a young girl in her trade. The title was *'L'Education Sentimentale'*. There was more on the same theme.

Press reaction was predictably hostile. Henceforth, Beardsley's contributions were closely scrutinised. A wary editorial eye was justified when John Lane spotted that an illustration labelled *The Fat Woman* might easily be taken as a caricature of the wife of James Whistler, an artist liable to call in the lawyers if he felt his reputation was impugned.

The storm was at its height when William Stone put the idea to Lane that he should move his office across Vigo Street to occupy apartment G.1 in Albany's ground floor. Part of the deal was for Lane to open up the bay window of the dining room to make an entrance directly on to Vigo Street. Any reservations the trustees might have had about bending the 'no business' rule were muted by the fact that for the past forty years the ponderous *Saturday Review* had been edited in G.1.

Lane took the opportunity of the move to break with his partner, Elkin Matthews, an antiquarian bookseller of mild disposition who could not keep up with Lane. It was later claimed by Lane that the split was mutual and amicable but it is closer to the truth to say that Lane made the running and that Elkin felt aggrieved, especially when Lane purloined the sign of The Bodley Head to rehang over his own doorway.

Caught up in the scandals of Oscar Wilde, Beardsley was dismissed from *The Yellow Book* which continued in diminished form until 1897. Beardsley died the following year, aged twenty-five. As for John Lane, riding the crest he had done so much to create, he achieved lasting fame with books that challenged literary norms. He died of pneumonia, aged sixty-nine in February 1925. Lane's nephew, Allen, led the paperback revolution of the 1930s and with his two brothers founded Penguin Books.

It might be wondered how William Stone allowed himself to be associated with radical publishing. But Stone was an eccentric with a sense of fun, one who delighted in doing things out of the ordinary. He was close on forty when he took three days to cycle from Albany to Penzance. A hot air balloon crossing of the Channel ended prematurely with a forced landing in Kent. A keen theatregoer, he was thrilled when an incident in his life inspired a play by Henry Arthur Jones, another resident of Albany. The plot turned on a treacherous valet who had adopted Stone's identity to run up a pile of debts.

In 1918 he moved home to Curzon Street to allow for space for his treasures, including a renowned butterfly collection. But he visited Albany every day, often calling in on his friend, the actor manager, Squire Bancroft, who occupied Stone's former apartment, A.1 with its high ceilings on three floors, the finest of the sixty-nine sets. Often recognised when he was out strolling, he cheerfully responded to the greetings of strangers who knew him as the Squire of Piccadilly.

With modernisation, Albany came back into favour. But a long waiting list was no guarantee of respectability. For the practised charlatan, a calling card with an Albany address was nine-tenths of credibility. A plausible rogue who this benefitted was William Redivivus Oliver de Lorncourt, Marquis de Leuville, otherwise known to his parents as Tom Oliver.

His step-father having paid for a European tour, young Tom settled in Paris where he acquired a titled wife who was on hard times. Back in London, *sans marquise*, he found rooms in Albany where his assumed identity came in handy for raising loans. He made the most of it.

> *The arms of the Leuvilles greeted one at every point; illuminated parchments, with heavy pendant seals, under bevelled glass and in Florentine frames, assured you that the Marquis's title had been bestowed upon his ancestors by all the kings and emperors of France from Charlemagne to Napoleon III. Even the fire-arms and door-knobs bore his arms.*

His appearance was equally outrageous.

> *Over the greasy locks that surmounted his fat, round, foolish face, he wore a huge silk sombrero, set at a rakish angle as if to indicate that he was rather a dog of a marquis.*

Even when he was exposed as a fake by Henry Labouchère, the campaigning editor of *Truth*, Leuville succeeded in reinventing himself as the literary adviser to the moderately well-off Mrs Peters of The Priory, Kilburn. Together they entertained and impressed aspiring romantic novelists. But the marquis could no longer afford Albany. In tandem with Mrs Peters, he retired to a small flat in Victoria Street while keeping up his pretence to grandeur.

Albany did not suit all tastes. 'A sombre and rather airless environment' said the diplomat and historian, Arthur Irwin Dasent, a view upheld by Simon Dewes:

> *If you come to Piccadilly to live, it has always seemed to me*
> *an odd thing that, as soon as you get there, you should try*
> *to shut yourself away as though you were in a village.*

But this was to underrate the attraction of Albany as a refuge for those on the run from marital discord or from an over-regulated home life. Into this last category fell Admiral of the Fleet, Sir Henry (Harry) Keppel, popularly known as the Little Admiral or the Grand Old Sailor. When asked why he had chosen rooms in Albany at the head of a long flight of stairs, when he had a perfectly good home to go to, he retorted, 'Jane can't get me here.' It was an open secret that Keppel's wife of thirty-four years was an intimidating lady.

Aged 95 at his death in 1904, the Admiral attributed his longevity to his brisk no-nonsense attitude to healthy living. When told that Gladstone, then in his eighties, was seriously ill, Keppel was unsympathetic.' If he would do as I do – climb up eighty steps, have a cold bath every day and sleep with his window always open – he would never be ill.'

Keppel lived modestly, surrounded by memories.

*The simple bed, with his earliest commission, signed by Nelson's flag-captain, Hardy, framed, over his head; engravings of Nelson's victories; photographs of the King and Queen, given 'to her beloved Little Admiral'; portraits of Coke of Norfolk and Sir Francis Burdett; Sir Dighton Probyn charging at the head of his splendid Lancers in the Indian Mutiny, and a hundred others.*

While his later life suggested a crusty misogynist, the Admiral was not devoid of romance. As a young naval officer he had come close to being cashiered for an 'indiscretion' with the wife of the governor of Cape Colony. A rather more positive achievement was to clear the waters of the Straits Settlements (Singapore, Malacca and Penang) of pirates. On his 90th birthday, Keppel decided to renew his acquaintance with the Straits. Despite family protests, he booked his passage to Singapore where he was given a hero's welcome. Singapore's new harbour, originally surveyed by Keppel, was named after him.

Of less fun than the Admiral or, rather, of no fun at all was the fifteenth Earl and second Marquess of Clanricarde, a mean-spirited and tight-fisted recluse who lived in Albany for forty-five years, from 1866 to 1911. Though he never visited his estates in Ireland, he squeezed every penny from his hard-pressed tenants and became a byword for parsimony. The only break in his drab life was an annual visit to St Leonards. Always staying at the same hotel, he was often mistaken for a wandering vagrant with barely enough money to pay for a meal. On one of his rare appearances at the House of Lords, he was detained at the entrance as a suspected anarchist.

The gay sub-culture that thrived in Piccadilly where casual sex in all its variations could be had at a price, inevitably had its overspill into Albany. While nerves were stretched by the trials of Oscar Wilde and by the 1898 amendment to the Vagrancy Act which criminalised men who 'in any public place persistently solicit or importune for immoral purposes', much was permitted within the bounds of discretion.

As a resident of Albany (set E.4) George Ives founded the Order of Chaeronea to bring together men seeking same sex relationships. A close friend of Oscar Wilde, he shared his bed with Lord Alfred Douglas, though he drew the line at a threesome because he 'thought it wouldn't do in the Albany', Ives urged restraint on Lord Alfred who was 'indulging in homosexuality to a reckless and highly dangerous degree' but lost interest when Douglas turned on Wilde.

With his lengthy association with Albany, Ives established a precedent. No longer was it necessary to demonstrate a strictly bachelor orientation to gain admission. Given the prevailing social bias, there were limits to be observed but the openly gay Albanian was no longer the exception.

During his time in Albany, Ives amassed a huge collection of press cuttings, case histories, letters and campaign notes relating to the cause dearest to his heart. These are now deposited with two American universities.

Is truth stranger than fiction? In the case of Albany, it is a close run thing. The cast of imaginary residents invented by novelists and playwrights, is arguably no odder than the roll call of those who really did live in Albany.

Setting the scene in The Bachelor of Albany, the Anglo-Irish writer, Marmion Savage, gave his acerbic description of Albany in mid-century as:

*The haunt of bachelors, or of married men who try to lead bachelors' lives – the dread of suspicious wives, the retreat of superannuated fops, the hospital for incurable oddities, a cluster of solitudes for social hermits, the home of homeless gentlemen, the diner-out and the diner-in, the place for the fashionable thrifty, the luxurious lonely, and the modish morose, the votaries of melancholy, and lovers of mutton-chops.*

Savage added:

*He knoweth not western London who is a stranger to the narrow arcade of chambers that forms a sort of private thoroughfare between Piccadilly and Burlington Gardens, guarded at each extremity by a fierce porter, or man-mastiff, whose duty it is to receive letters, cards, and parcels, and repulse intrusive wives, disagreeable fathers, and importunate tradesmen.*

It all sounded rather sinister. Charles Dickens added his dose of vitriol. In *Our Mutual Friend* (1864), he puts Fledgeby, corrupt moneylender and man about town, in Albany. When Jenny Wren, a crippled dressmaker arrives by appointment, she is received by a fearsome housekeeper.

*'You want someone?' said the lady in a stern manner.*

*'I am going upstairs to Mr. Fledgeby's.'*

*'You cannot do that at this moment, there is a gentleman with him. I am waiting for the gentleman. His business with Mr. Fledgeby will very soon be transacted, and then you can go up. Until the gentleman comes down, you must wait here.'*

*The gentleman's 'business' was to administer Fledgeby a terrible thrashing. Jenny heard a kind of spluttering, and someone beating a carpet, and some odd noises.*

*Soon afterwards, came a slamming and banging of doors; and then came running downstairs a gentleman with whiskers, and out of breath, who seemed to be red hot.*

*'Is your business done, Alfred?' inquired the lady.*

*'Very thoroughly done,' replied the gentleman, as he took his hat from her.*

*'You can go up to Mr. Fledgeby as soon as you like,' said the lady, moving haughtily away.*

*'Oh! And you can take these three pieces of stick with you,' added the gentleman, politely.*

On a milder note, Lord Lufton in Anthony Trollope's *Framley Parsonage* (1864) lived in Albany as did a character in Oscar Wilde's first triumph, *The Picture of Dorian Gray* (1890). Five years later, Wilde gave Ernest, the raffish alter ego of John Worthing, an Albany apartment in *The Importance of Being Earnest*. In the original version of the play Miss Prism declared the 'wicked' Ernest to be 'as bad as any young man who had chambers in The Albany or, indeed in the vicinity of Piccadilly can possibly be'. The slight was cut from the performed script.

Choosing Albany as the home of the upper crust Aubrey Tanqueray in his stage drama, *The Second Mrs Tanqueray*, Sir Arthur Wing Pinero visualised 'a richly and tastefully decorated room elegantly and luxuriously furnished: on the right a large pair of doors opening into another room, on the left at the further end of the room a small door leading to a bedchamber. A circular table is laid for dinner for four persons, which has not reached the stage of dessert and coffee. Everything in the apartment suggests wealth and refinement. The fire is burning brightly.'

Albany seems to have a particular attraction for crime writers. A.J. Raffles, the gentleman thief created by E.W. Hornung in the late 1890s, set up his nefarious business in Albany along with Bunny, his very close chum, who acts as a narrator for their daring escapades. Apparently, Hornung never recognised the implications of a male relationship that was quite so intimate.

Anthony Berkeley, a recently rediscovered author from the golden age of crime fiction, gave Albany as the address for his bachelor sleuth, Roger Sheringham (*Murder in the Basement*, 1932) while on the other side of law and order, the chief suspect in Henry Wade's crime mystery, *The Verdict of You All* (1939) was also in residence. Wade himself (real name Major Sir Henry Lancelot Aubrey-Fletcher, 6th Baronet KStJ CVO DSO), a veteran of the Great War, would have felt entirely at home in Albany.

Inevitably, P.G. Wodehouse, who lived in a luxury pad off Park Lane, chose Albany as an ideal habitat for his upper class drones. This is where we find Pongo Twistleton, nephew of Lord Ickenham and fall guy for the mad escapades of the sprightly old Earl. Pongo had to move out when he married Sally Painter.

In *Sinister Street* (1913), Compton Mackenzie came closest to the ideal promoted by the doyens of Albany when he described a visit by Michael Fane to his late father's friend Prescott, a bachelor soldier. He 'enjoyed the darkness of the room whose life seemed to radiate from the gleaming table in its centre. He enjoyed the ghostly motions of the soldier-servant and the half-obscured vision of stern old prints on the walls of the great square room, and he enjoyed the intense silence that brooded outside the heavily-curtained windows.'

The dozen or so other writers who have introduced Albany into their work range from John Buchan to Conan Doyle who described Albany as 'an aristocratic rookery'. The wide coverage suggests that the trustees' obsession with privacy is counterproductive.

# 14
# Piccadilly Plus and Minus

The plus was the Ritz, described by critic Marcus Binney as 'one of the all-time masterpieces of hotel architecture'. It gave a distinction to Piccadilly that was hard to match though many have tried.

The Ritz was something new in Piccadilly experience. Decent hotels hardly existed in nineteenth century London. In the late 1860s when, after the death of Prince Albert, there was pressure on the Queen to take a more active role in public life, *The Times* urged that visiting foreign notables should be accommodated in Buckingham Palace, London hotels being so bad 'they had become nothing more than a refuge for the homeless'. 'Rich Americans', said the restaurant critic Lieut-Col Newnham-Davis, 'looked on London as a Clapham Junction, a necessary but disagreeable halting place on the way to Paris.'

Basic accommodation could be had at the Clarendon in New Bond Street best known for its chef, Monsieur Jacquier, who had cooked for Louis XVIII before moving to London to become an early promoter of French cuisine.

The Ritz, a magnet for the rich and famous

Setting a higher standard was the Pulteney at 105 Piccadilly. Taking its name from the family of the Earls of Bath who had a long record as West End landowners, the opening of the Pulteney occurred at around the time of the defeat of Napoleon at Waterloo. The timing was auspicious since European dignitaries needed somewhere to stay in London when they turned up for the victory celebration. While renting a house was generally the preferred alternative to risking a hotel, Czar Alexander I decided to favour the Pulteney. His appearance on the balcony to greet the

London sightseers delighted the hotel manager, John Escudier, who knew the value of celebrity endorsement.

The location of the Pulteney on the edge of a busy thorough-fare, limited its attraction. When the four Caton sisters, American heiresses, stayed there on the first round of their strategy to marry into the British aristocracy (an objective they speedily achieved) the noise day and night was intolerable.

> *There was no rest to be had there. At first, the sisters took a suite of rooms arranged with their bedchambers at the back overlooking the mews. Over the cobblestones from about half-past six every morning came the dust carts with their bells and the dustmen with their chants of 'Dust-ho'. Then came the porterhouse carts rattling with pewter pots; then the milk carts and then the vegetable sellers so that a succession of cries, each in a different tone, so numerous when mixed with the stables housed there ... meant there was an unholy noise throughout the morning.*

In 1823, the Pulteney moved from Piccadilly to Albemarle Street where it raised its game by becoming one of the first hotels to introduce flush toilets. On its former site was built Bath House, a Piccadilly mansion of no great distinction. Occupied by a succession of the mega rich, the site was cleared in 1960.

A leap forward in hotel standards came in the 1880s with the building of the Savoy in the Strand. This state-of-the art creation with electric light throughout, 'ascending rooms' or lifts, private bathrooms (at a supplementary price) and hot and cold running water (hitherto hot water was provided only when requested) was the brainchild of Richard D'Oyly Carte who made his fortune as the producer of the Gilbert and Sullivan operas. To manage his luxury hotel, he headhunted César Ritz as manager and Auguste Escoffier, one of the greatest chefs of his generation, to be in charge of the kitchens.

Ritz was already close to the peak of his profession. Born into a family of Swiss peasant farmers, he had started out as an apprentice wine waiter. It had not lasted long. At the end of a year, his employer told him he lacked the 'special flair' that made for success in the restaurant business. Undaunted, Ritz set off for Paris where he found work as a waiter in a fashionable restaurant.

A quick learner, Ritz progressed to be restaurant manager at the Grand Hotel in Nice. Now well on the way to an illustrious career, his progress was accelerated by his association with Auguste Escoffier. Together, they opened a restaurant in Baden-Baden, a favourite health spa.

With his reputation for refinement and elegance, Ritz was the obvious choice to bring D'Oyly Carte's dream to realisation.

Recalling Ritz in his days at the Savoy, Lieut-Col Newnham-Davis described him

> *... as very slim, very quiet with nervous hands clasped tightly together; he would move through the big restaurant seeing everything ... bowing to some of the diners, standing by a table to speak to others, possessing a marvellous knowledge of faces and of what the interests were of all the important people of his clientèle.*

*Newnham-Davis went on, 'Ritz had an enormous facility*
*for quick work, no detail was too small for him and when*
*he had made up his mind that a thing should be done he*
*took unlimited trouble to have it carried out.'*

The collaboration with D'Oyly Carte lasted for seven highly profitable years – Carte making more money from his hotel than from
any of his theatrical enterprises. But it was only a matter of time
before two meteoric egos collided.

The explosion was over the misplacement – Carte called it a
misappropriation – of a quantity of wine and spirits. Carte also
claimed to have evidence of kickbacks from suppliers though it
is hard to imagine that he was shocked at an almost universal
practice in the hotel and restaurant trade. Handed his dismissal
notice, Ritz contemplated legal action but was dissuaded by
Escoffier who urged a more constructive form of retaliation by
outmatching Carte's grandiose schemes.

There proved to be no problem in attracting finance. With
the backing of Alfred Beit, the South African gold and diamond
mogul, one of the world's richest men, Ritz and Escoffier decamped to Paris where the Ritz Hotel opened to universal acclaim. But Ritz had still to stamp his imprint on London where
he was determined to outshine all his earlier achievements.

With the rebuilding of Her Majesty's Theatre at the Pall Mall
end of the Haymarket, the proposal for a new hotel alongside
was snapped up by Ritz. Built in the French Renaissance style, a
near replica of Her Majesty's, the hotel, to be called the Carlton,
was designed to outclass the Savoy. As a measure of his success,

many of the Savoy's regular clients, including the Prince of Wales (Edward VII), transferred their allegiance to the Carlton which was judged to offer the best food and the best service with décor distinguished by Ritz's famous palms. Badly damaged in the 1940 Blitz, the Carlton was eventually demolished to make way for New Zealand's High Commission.

A big disappointment for Ritz came in 1902 with cancellation of the coronation of Edward VII. When the king fell ill and the coronation postponed, Ritz, who had been working frenetically to put the Carlton at the heart of the celebrations, suffered a breakdown. He retired temporarily leaving Escoffier in charge.

A contributory factor in Ritz's collapse was the competition he now faced from D'Oyly Carte's latest venture, the Berkeley Hotel on the corner of Piccadilly and Berkeley Street. Originally known as the Gloucester Coffee House, to serve mail-coach passengers heading for the West Country, Carte restyled the premises to rival the Carlton. Opened in 1901, the Berkeley was to remain in place until it moved to Knightsbridge.

Revived after an extended rest, Ritz responded to the challenge of the Berkeley with the boldest move of his career. Almost opposite the Berkeley, close to Green Park where once stood The Old White Horse Cellar, another of Piccadilly's famous coaching inns, was the Bath Hotel and the Walsingham House Hotel, the latter not so much a hotel in the conventional sense but more a block of luxury mansion flats, almost certainly inspired by Albany. Lord Walsingham, who had put up the money for the eight storey building, reserved one of the apartments for his private use.

Neither he nor his tenants were long in residence. Completed in 1887, the life of Walsingham House was cut short by César Ritz. With backers for whom money was no object, he bought Walsingham House and the Bath Hotel with the aim of clearing the entire site for his jewel in the Piccadilly crown.

The architect for the London Ritz was Charles Mewès, an outsized personality but with a limited command of English. To compensate, he relied on Arthur Davis, his young, bilingual partner who had been born in London but brought up in Brussels. Fastidiously neat and something of a dandy, Davis was an expert on good food and wine. Both architects had worked on the Paris Ritz and on the Carlton and were responsible for the Royal Automobile Club in Pall Mall.

With 'grand vistas, lofty proportions and sparkling chandeliers, the Ritz,' says Binney, 'is a brilliant marriage of Ritz's own formula for a grand yet intimate interior and the Beaux-Arts training of both Mewès and Davis. Beaux-Arts architects relished the play of unusual shapes – circles, octagons and ovals – in a ground plan, and the London Ritz has all of these. As leading motifs, it has two especially French features – the grand axis and the framed vista. Mewès and Davis had seized the opportunity offered by the steel frame to create an open layout that runs the length of the hotel from the Arlington Street entrance to the Restaurant overlooking Green Park.

The arcade on the Piccadilly side or the hotel, inspired by the rue de Rivoli in Paris, had the practical advantage of providing extra space for the bedrooms above.

'As to the restaurant,' adds Binney, 'it is not only one of the most beautiful interiors in London, it can be claimed as the most beautiful hotel restaurant in the world. Davis's genius lay in creating a room that is as ravishing by night as by day, that at once grand and intimate, ornate, yet restful to the eye.'

A year before the official opening on May 24th, 1906, the press gave the Ritz ecstatic reviews to the interior of London's first free standing, steel-framed building. *The Graphic* rhapsodised on a hotel that is 'the high watermark of convenience, beauty and comfort'. Every bedroom had an open fireplace and, an oddity to modern eyes, a copper coal scuttle shaped like a classic urn. Among the many luxury aids available to guests were silver-plated tongs for stretching the fingers of wet gloves. Spacious bathrooms with glazed tiles were all supplied with running hot water and showers, still a novelty at the time except for wealthy Americans. With his close attention to spotlessly clean surroundings, Ritz set the trend for private residences springing up in what were then the outlying parts of the capital.

As chef, Monsieur Malley, a star of the Paris Ritz, transferred his talents to London. Malley had the reputation for inventing new and memorable dishes such as salmon with a crayfish mousse. His cakes were so much enjoyed by Edward VII, he had regular supplies sent to him at Buckingham Palace.

After the London Ritz was firmly on the map, its creator gradually withdrew from the business, finally retiring in 1911. His wife attributed his decline to overwork but in reality he was a victim of dementia.

Of the fund of stories linked to the great and good patrons of The Ritz, one of the least well-known is the curious tale of the porters' desk. This massive mahogany crescent, dominating the foyer, was taken out of service in 1987 as part of a refurbishment. At the back, below a gap between the desk and the wall, was found a treasure trove of lost postcards, letters, leaflets and notes, a century's worth of forgotten clutter. Contained within this time capsule were timetables for river-trips of 1922, car-hire rate cards from 1930, when it cost a guinea for two hours or ten miles in a Daimler, a collection of come-hither photographs of actress Juliette Margel appearing at the Adelphi Theatre in 1912 and a bill run up by Sydney Smith in 1908 for a straw boater (price eight shillings and six pence). The most poignant memento was a love letter ('Oh Darling I am so hungry to see you again, just for a moment or two ...'), ardent but forever unappreciated.

The success of the Ritz inspired imitators. For entrepreneurs with an eye on the future, there were attractive properties ripe for conversion coming on to the market. The reason was not hard to find. For the nobility, the attractions of a mansion with spacious grounds in central London were fast losing their charm.

The imports of cheap American grain had cut sharply into the income of the landed gentry while death duties, introduced in 1894 and rising to fifteen per cent on inherited fortunes over £1 million in 1907, had further eroded the aristocratic entitlement. Moreover, the entire West End was changing character as it became more commercialised. In 1895, the Earl of Harewood sold his Adam-designed mansion in Hanover Square to the

Royal Agricultural Society. Having stood empty for twenty years, Harcourt House in Cavendish Square was pulled down in 1906.

If residential Piccadilly had any attraction at all, it was chiefly to the *nouveaux riches*. The bookmaker, speculator and philanthropist, George Herring, lived at Number 141 while his neighbour at 143 was Sir William Coddington, the Lancashire cotton mogul. His close neighbour was Hamar Bass of the Burton Brewing dynasty.

The Great War took a further knock at those who depended on inherited wealth. In 1919, death duties were raised to forty per cent on estates of over £2 million. Even allowing for loopholes in the legislation that enrolled clever accountants to reduce the burden, the impact could be traumatic. Add to this the rising cost of hiring domestic staff who were easily tempted into better paid and more congenial employment, it is easy to see why the old money was in retreat.

An exception was the Duke of York, later George VI. He and his family moved into 145 Piccadilly, then a spacious mansion, in 1926. One of his two daughters, Princess Elizabeth, was destined to be Queen Elizabeth II. Immune from taxation and with no money problems, the Yorks were able to support a full staff including a butcher and under butcher, a telephonist, two footmen, a valet, a dresser, a cook, two kitchen maids, a night watchman and a Royal Air Force orderly as a general dogsbody.

Piccadilly was not to the liking of Princess Elizabeth. She was happiest in the York's second house, the Royal Lodge in Windsor Great Park where, in 98 acres of pasture and woodland, she could nurture her love of animals and all things rural. After the abdication of Edward VIII and the accession of George VI, the family migrated across the park to Buckingham Palace. 145 Piccadilly fell to a German bomb in 1940 and is now the site of the Intercontinental Hotel which fronts on to Park Lane.

Where the Ritz led, a middle class imitation with rooms at affordable rates, soon followed. Inevitably, it was Joe Lyons who took the initiative. The Strand Palace Hotel was quickly followed in 1915 by the Regent Palace Hotel on Piccadilly Circus. With 1,028 bedrooms, albeit without bathrooms, it was Europe's largest hotel. Given a boost by London's post-war tourism, it entered its long decline in the 1950s (cheap rooms, no questions asked) and was eventually demolished in 2010. Part of the site is now Zedel, a Parisian-style brasserie.

If the Ritz was a mighty plus for Piccadilly, the corresponding minus was the destruction of Devonshire House. Made famous by Georgiana, the vibrant Duchess of Devonshire, social and political superstar of late eighteenth century Piccadilly, Devonshire House had subsequently a chequered history. Empty, apart from the servants for long periods, it came into its own for grand events such as the ball given to celebrate Queen Victoria's Jubilee in 1897 and for occasional theatrical extravaganzas to raise money for charity.

A political connection was provided by the 8th Duke who succeeded to the title in 1891. The epitome of the perfect country gentleman, the Duke took seriously his senior roles in successive governments. But his heart was not in it. When the Tory Party led by the cerebral Arthur Balfour was convulsed over the relative merits of free trade and protection, Devonshire struggled to understand the economic intricacies. He had no pretensions. Asked how he had reacted to one of Balfour's frequent letters urging his support, one of the family declared that 'as yet it has not been taken out of the bottom of his shooting coat'. In his exchanges in the House of Lords, he was a model for Lord Emsworth, the woolly-minded peer created by P.G. Wodehouse. Listening to one of his fellow peers proclaiming 'the proudest moment' of his life, the Duke responded in a loud aside, 'The proudest moment in my life was when my pig won the first prize at Skipton Fair'.

The Duke died in Cannes in 1908. His heir, the 9th Duke, saddled with death duties and family debts, decided it was time to sever the Devonshire connection with Piccadilly. In more propitious times, Devonshire House would almost certainly have survived under a new aegis. With its three acres of land, it would easily have converted to a university college, national museum, or art gallery. But in the 1920s, in a country still struggling to adapt to a post-war economy, with a government beholden to false economies, there was no interest in spending to preserve what was generally regarded as a mighty albatross. To London's everlasting shame, the philistines moved in. When Devonshire House was sold for just over £1 million, the buyers, Lawrence Harrison and Shurmer Sibthorpe, made no secret of their intention to clear the site for offices and showrooms. Said the unenlightened Sibthorpe, 'Archaeologists' (he presumably meant conservationists) 'have gathered round me to say I am a vandal but personally I think the place is an eyesore.' The wreckers took over.

The Mayfair Hotel now stands on what was once part of the Devonshire House garden. The only reminder of a once noble residence are the iron gates which were moved across Piccadilly to mark the entrance to Green Park.

The extensive rebuilding of Piccadilly and Regent Street early in the twentieth century was partly motivated by business interests, partly by a government-inspired ambition to raise the profile of London to match the grandeur of Paris and Berlin. The objective, said Prime Minister Arthur Balfour, was to create a 'monumental ensemble of the kind which other nations have shown example and which we may well imitate and can easily surpass'. The result, unveiled between 1906 and 1913 was a widening of the Mall, the building of Admiralty Arch and the transformation of Buckingham Palace with a Portland stone façade, made more imposing by putting the Victoria Monument in front of the main gates.

Next for updating in sturdy imperial style, impressive generally but uninspiring, was the whole of Regent Street. Nearly all the major buildings seen today are from the 1920s. Only to the north, by Regent's Park, are there any survivals from the age of John Nash. That said, Regent Street still follows the same gentle curve designed by Nash to link with Piccadilly Circus.

The new face of Regent Street was unveiled in 1927 with a royal dedication by George V. Press comments were mostly favourable to a wider thoroughfare allowing for the free movement of motorised traffic. But architectural critics were less impressed. John Betjeman was of those who regretted the passing of the elegant Nash stucco in favour of 'greying, dreary stone [with buildings] far too high for the width of the roadway'.

The reconstituted Café Royal was 'no longer the likeable ne'er-do-well which we used to know', complained the

*Architectural Review*. 'It no longer suggests the gaudy and smoky room ... where Englishmen could enjoy the luxury of forgetting that they must always behave like gentlemen.'

The evolution of Piccadilly was more piecemeal. The Ritz and the Piccadilly Hotel dominated the two ends of the stately boulevard. Next to the Ritz, William Curtis Brown, the classical architect, was responsible for the Wolseley showroom for what, pre-war, was one of Britain's top selling luxury cars. That was in 1922. Four years later, Curtis Brown converted the building to suit the requirements of Barclays Bank while opposite he created a home for the National Westminster Bank. The interiors were noted for their grand marble pillars and archways. Today, the Wolseley is a fashionable restaurant, until recently managed by Chris Corbin and Jeremy King, the partnership that transformed London's restaurant scene.

About midway on Piccadilly, two mighty insurance companies faced each other across the street. From 1910, the sturdy building that housed the Royal Insurance stood opposite the equally sturdy Norwich Union. A rarely noted feature of the latter is the sculptures, set too high for easy observation, of a hooded figure of justice holding the scales of justice flanked by two crouched scantily-dressed male and female figures representing prudence and a secure future. More elegant was Edward Lutyens's design for a branch of the Midland Bank at 196 Piccadilly on the corner of St James's Churchyard. Finished in 1922, it was inspired by Sanmicheli's Porta San Zeno at Verona. It is now, Maison Assouline, a prestige bookshop and elegant bar.

Across from the Burlington Arcade was built the Piccadilly Arcade linking to Jermyn Street. Starting as a cinema on a rather grand scale in 1926 it was converted into a shopping mall. An outstanding feature is the curved glass windows. Ian Nairn, an architectural critic who was hard to please, wrote lyrically of 'the bows, fifteen to twenty feet high ... they ripple down the slope from Piccadilly like the sides of a Greek temple all done in glass.'

The outstanding expression of the modern spirit was Simpsons, the showcase for one of Britain's leading ready-to-wear tailors. A few steps from the Circus, the building is now the largest of the Waterstone's chain of bookstores. But while it has been adapted for its new role, the distinction of the original remains intact, as does the Simpson's sign set in stone on each side of the entrance.

The Simpson story, from rags to riches, began in 1897 in Petticoat Lane, the East End centre of the garment trade, with a young tailor by name of Simeon Simpson. With a reputation for quality tailoring and an eye for adopting labour-saving technology, it was not long before he was expanding the business to cater for clients across the country. His proud boast was to be able to complete and dispatch a suit within twenty-four hours of receiving the order. The Simpson workshop was upgraded to a Simpson factory. Opening in 1929 in Stoke Newington, the factory had a three thousand strong workforce turning out 11,000 garments a day. By now, Simeon's youngest son, Alexander was active in the firm and it was he who took on the next challenge, that of finding a site in central London for a Simpson store.

In the spring of 1935, the Crown Commissioners invited offers for the abandoned Geological Museum, a few steps away from Piccadilly Circus. With a frontage of seventy-one feet to Piccadilly and the same to Jermyn Street, a ground area of about eleven thousand square feet was waiting to be occupied by a building of 'handsome architectural design ... faced in Portland stone approved by the Commissioners.' Alec Simpson was only too happy to oblige. Doubtless his successful bid was partly motivated by the proximity of Austin Reed, Simpson's great rival, nearby in Regent Street.

Stepping in as the Simpson architect, Joseph Emberton was a thoroughgoing modernist, much influenced by Scandinavian and German design that called for bold, clean lines, light and space, a satisfying amalgam of practicality and beauty.

> *The main elements of the store ... were clearly established from the first: the great bands of window on Piccadilly and Jermyn Street; the vertical window rising floor to ceiling by the immense central marble staircase, providing daylight to the midst of each floor; the unimpeded open floors, from front to back; the non-reflecting concave windows at street level – all these were among the first ideas proposed by Emberton, and immediately agreed by Alec Simpson.*

Simpson's Piccadilly was distinguished by innovation. A steel-framed building made extensive use of chromium plate, in commercial use for less than a decade, and natural woods. Neon light strips were fitted for night illumination. For the interior, Alec tapped into the Bauhaus school of design led by Walter Gropius whose objective was 'to liberate the creative artist from his otherworldliness and reintegrate him into the workaday world of realities; and at the same time to broaden and humanize the rigid, almost exclusively material mind of the businessman.'

Alec Simpson was all for that. To work on display ideas he engaged Lazlo Moholy-Nagy, a Hungarian-born refugee from Nazi Germany who had taught at the Bauhaus. For the opening, Moholy-Nagy planned an animation exhibition (the universally recognised symbol of modernism) with three aircraft for inspection on the fifth floor. The press coverage was satisfyingly extensive. For the official opening on April 29th, 1936, the ribbon was cut by Sir Malcolm Campbell, the holder of the world land speed record.

The impeccably-dressed men and women, smart but relaxed in work and play, who became the mainstay of Simpson advertising, sprang from the lively imagination of Max Hoff, an Austrian artist and designer, another escapee from Nazi persecution. Adopted by Simpson outlets across the country, the distinctive image became almost a cliché of the tailoring ideal.

The Simpson success story was unimpeded for a half century. But by the 1980s, the style revolution led by a younger generation, no longer content to be dressed like their parents, took its toll on the bottom line. Too small to be a department store and too large to be a speciality store, Simpson's Piccadilly closed its doors for the last time in 1998.

# 15
# War and Peace

When war broke out in 1939, aerial attacks put London in the front line. While Docklands and the East End suffered the worst of the Blitz, 'up West' was not immune.

In one of the worst raids of the war, James Lees-Milne took refuge in the Piccadilly Hotel where in the entrance hall 'slices of thick plain glass were strewn upon the carpet'.

Two bombs struck the hotel.

*While the foundations rocked and swayed there was time to screw my body like a hedgehog into a protective ball against the masonry crumbling, rumbling down the marble staircase. Were we to be crushed, buried alive, underground? A cataract of boulders was arrested by a grand piano. A smashing, slashing of glass and wood followed in its wake. Nothing further. The lights went out. Officious men's voices shouted, 'Keep calm!' Everyone kept calm. There was a stifling smell of cordite and the acrid stench of plaster and stale wallpaper. When torches were flashed on nothing was visible but blobs of light behind a fog of black, curling smoke.*

Victory in Europe, Piccadilly Circus, May 8, 1945

Emerging into the street after the 'all-clear', Lees-Milne found 'the contents of shop windows strewn over the pavement'. Outside a jewellers, he picked up a handful of precious stones to 'chuck them back into the shop before they got trodden on, or looted.'

A high-explosive bomb bursting at the north end of Burlington Arcade demolished five shops. St James's Church took a direct hit, leaving it a spireless shell. Albany was hit twice, the second time by an incendiary bomb which all but destroyed G block.

Writer and translator, Clifford Bax was out of town when his Albany apartment was hit. Returning to assess the damage, he got no further than Vigo Street.

*That bedroom window, desolately open, had little glass left
in it. The high bow-window, on the farther side of which
I had worked so happily for eight years, still carried most
of the criss-cross paper which I had put up there on the day
when Poland was invaded, and on my derelict balcony the
peace-time creepers were still creeping, indifferent to the
presence in their world of Homo sapiens.*

Bax was not down-hearted.

*A new phase of life had been forced upon me and, turning
away, I recognised that humanity was rapidly advancing,
in its blind manner, towards a new phase of social life.*

The actress Edith Evans was another Albany resident who was
equally phlegmatic. Now remembered chiefly for her signature
role as Lady Bracknell in *The Importance of Being Earnest* (happily
preserved in an otherwise indifferent movie adaptation), Dame
Edith, as she became in 1946, was essentially a loner. More or less
contentedly married to an absentee husband (they exchanged occasional loving letters) she did not court publicity and had few
close friends. Albany was perfect for her. Her set of chambers was
L.4, immediately opposite J.B. Priestley who, like Edith, stayed
on in London throughout the Blitz, in his case to make a series of
memorable broadcasts that were as inspirational, though totally
different in tone and context, to those of Winston Churchill.

She did canteen work after she left the theatre and was often
trapped there until the All Clear sounded in the early hours. She
enjoyed telling of the time when, in the blackout, she assured a

close friend that the route to the underground cellar in Albany was 'quite flat right through'. It wasn't anything of the sort.

> *There were about seven steps and she went headlong. Awful, she never let me forget it. I mean, I did more damage to her than Hitler. I couldn't stick all those people trooping down to the shelter about nine o'clock every night and starting to go to sleep. Nobody talked, or told any jokes, or anything. It was awfully boring, I thought. Some of them had their coffee brought down by their parlourmaids. That used to make me roar with laughter. I didn't go all that often, only when things got really bad. They dropped a bomb just across the road, on that lovely church in Piccadilly, and that did us all some damage, but most nights I couldn't be bothered.*

Eat, drink and be merry was the philosophy of the young men in uniform who congregated in Piccadilly. With more than a million American troops in Britain in the lead-up to D-Day, Piccadilly was another Manhattan. Remaining open all night, Lyons Popular Café was handed over to the Americans where they were entertained by stars of stage and screen.

As in the past, prostitution thrived. The nightly parade of sex workers was along Piccadilly, up Bond Street, round by Burlington Gardens and down to Piccadilly again via Sackville Street. The super coquettes, called Piccadilly Commandos or Hyde Park Rangers, many of them French refugees, congregated near the Ritz. Commented the drama critic James Agate, 'How are the fallen mighty' GIs were charged at the highest rate while their counterparts, on lower pay, were given a discount. One veteran sex worker reported a 14-hour day catering for nearly fifty clients.

The Piccadilly celebration that came closest to the Relief of Mafeking was for Victory in Europe, V.E. Day, 1945. All roads into the Circus were closed to traffic and a bonfire was lit in Haymarket. Amateur rock climbers competed to be first to sit on top of the pyramid structure protecting Eros's pedestal. Eros himself was not there to preside over the fun. He had been packed off to Egham in Surrey for the duration and did not return to his perch until 1948.

After the party, came the hangover. Post-war London was a dreary place. Everywhere there were bomb sites with piles of rubble wanting to be cleared, often to make way for parking lots.

> *Buildings black with soot cried out for a lick of paint.*
> *Boarded-up windows presented a blank face to the world.*
> *... the people looked tired and worn. Women holding string*
> *bags stood patiently in long lines outside shops, resignation*
> *on their faces. If he closed his eyes the visitor became more*
> *conscious of the all-pervasive smell. It was of coal smoke in*
> *the damp chill, but something else too. Dust! Dust so acrid*
> *you could taste it in your mouth.*

There were plans galore for giving Piccadilly Circus a facelift. That it was long overdue was a cliché of professional and political debate. Few dissented from the view of Sir Reginald Blomfield that the Circus was nothing more than a 'disorderly rabble of buildings which at present disgraced the most important place in London'. But this was to miss the point. The 'disorderly rabble' was precisely what gave the Circus an anarchic sense of fun, a magnet for the many who wanted an escape from their orderly, tedious lives to gather in a spot that encouraged affection rather than sober respect.

The planners made the fundamental mistake of wanting everything neat and tidy in line with uniform rules of development. Thus, the perfectly laudable aim of the 1945 County of London Plan to make more of the West End 'available for housing for people of moderate means' was to be given practical shape in the building of hideous tower blocks such as the 1960s Kemp House in Berwick Street.

The second planning error was to assume that the car would forever be king. With the free movement of traffic as the first consideration, pedestrians were to be handed a new deal.

The distance between the planners' vision and what ordinary people wanted was demonstrated when, after more than a decade of blackout, the Piccadilly Circus lights came on again in 1949. While Sir Patrick Abercrombie, the guru of post-war planning, described the Circus as a neon hell, the crowds of delighted sightseers bringing traffic to a halt was a bright spot in the otherwise grey world of post-war austerity.

The planners who sought order from chaos would have deserved more sympathy had they not fallen for the sales pitch of cowboy developers with vapid architects in tow. For Piccadilly, the nadir was reached in 1959 when the LCC granted an application from Jack Cotton, 'a master salesman', to erect a thirteen-storey, 172-foot high building, much of it windowless, on the Monico site in Piccadilly Circus. Shops, offices and restaurants were to be dwarfed by illuminated advertisements. A dominant feature of this excrescence was a crane, with a reach of ninety-three feet, to change the electrical signs. Yet so confident was Cotton of getting his way with the LCC, whose chief architect had cooperated with Cotton to produce an acceptable scheme, that he jumped the gun by sharing with the press his Piccadilly fantasy. Cotton found himself up against The Fine Arts Civic Trust, a body concerned with more responsible planning. But it was the uniform hostility of the press that made all the difference, one critic calling the design 'a ribald monstrosity' and another describing it as 'a greedy, tasteless, lumpy, clumping, squat tower on an amorphous podium'. Writing in *The Spectator*, Bernard Levin, an acerbic political commentator, went for the jugular. Condemning the 'monster of Piccadilly', Levin made a direct attack on Cotton as a property speculator with few scruples. Of Cotton's architects, Cotton, Ballard and Blow, Levin pointed out that Cotton had no architectural qualifications, that Blow was a registered (not chartered) architect, and that Ballard was dead.

The whole undertaking being referred to the Minister of Town and Country Planning, a public inquiry was ordered. The report concluded that 'the present project and the planning purposes for which it was associated did not make the best of the opportunity ... unfolding for Piccadilly Circus'. Permission for the development was refused with the rider, implied rather than boldly stated, that the future of Piccadilly should not be left to the mercy of property speculators. The political consensus was to hand over the problem to 'a single architectural mind', a return to the days of Norman Shaw and Reginald Blomfield.

The chalice was passed to Sir William Holford (later Baron Holford, the first town planner to be raised to the peerage). For all his distinction, Holford shared the failing of most of his contemporaries, of giving too much regard to the car as the embodiment of modernism. A succession of his plans for the Circus had one thing in common, the creation of a piazza for pedestrians above ground-level traffic. Eros was to be raised aloft on a pedestal surrounded by office towers. The new space was to be distinguished by a 'very slim vertical feature' topped by a finial in the form of a 'ruff' as a symbol of Piccadilly origins. That Holford had no luck in selling his proposals to the government is in no way any credit to the politicians. When, at the end of the 1960s, Holford's latest proposal was rejected it was, incredibly, because it only allowed for a twenty per cent increase in traffic. The government wanted a fifty per cent increase.

If there was anywhere that kept the flame burning for old Piccadilly, it was Albany. The rules were still strict – no pets, no children, no whistling, no noise and absolutely, no publicity. Above all else, privacy was prized by Albanians. No surprise there. It was remarkable that of the sixty-nine flats, so many were occupied by oddballs.

Of the post-war cadre, Donald Downes, a large American with a booming voice, was Albany's leading man of mystery. Having served Allied interests by infiltrating the German backed America First Committee, he joined the Office of Strategic Services, the US intelligence agency, to double as a war correspondent in North Africa, Cairo and, finally, in Italy where he witnessed the last days of the Mussolini regime. It was there that he met the young, handsome future theatre and movie director, Franco Zeffirelli whom he immediately engaged as an interpreter.

The justification was weak since Downes spoke near perfect Italian but he had a sharp eye for good-looking young men.

Zeffirelli became devoted to the ebullient maverick though, by his account, there was never any suggestion of a sexual relationship. With the end of the war, Downes settled with his long term companion, Bob Ullman, in a villa with a spectacular view over the bay to Positano.

> *They really were 'the odd couple'. Although never anything but friends, theirs was a sort of marriage. They bickered the whole time and quarrelled about everything from food to the books with which the villa was piled high – Donald read about three a day. But if anyone else dared criticize the one to the other, then let the third party beware. To the outside world they presented a united front. It was a unique household, a mixture of culture and eccentricity. There was a constant stream of literary and theatre folk. There were bizarre fads like Donald's sudden aggressive dieting, or excessive feasting, which meant that he had to have three entire wardrobes for when he was thin, fat or just in-between.*

When Ullman was killed in a car crash, Downes moved to Albany though with help from Zeffirelli, he kept his villa which eventually passed to his now successful friend from the war years.

Though discreet about his secret service activities, Downes lived an openly gay life ever eager to help friends in need such as the homosexual Tory MP, Martin Stevens, who lodged with Downes after getting into money troubles.

Of the top lawyers who lived in Albany, of fondest memory is Sir Patrick Hastings, in residence from 1948 to the year of his death in 1952. Hastings was multi-talented. He made his name as a deadly cross-examiner in a succession of high-profile cases. He won damages for his friend Edgar Wallace when he was accused of plagiarism; he did the same for the Russian aristocrat wife of Rasputin's killer, libelled in a Hollywood film *Rasputin the Mad Monk*; he secured the acquittal of a well-known socialite, Elvira Barney, for the murder of her lover; and he was twice successful on behalf of Sir Oswald Mosley, then at the height of his rabble-rousing powers, first winning substantial libel damages against the *Star* newspaper, and second on a charge of riotous assembly.

As a politician (he was first elected in 1922) he held office as Attorney General in the 1924 Labour government headed by Ramsay MacDonald, a prime minister who found it hard to grasp essentials. But it was Hastings who, ill-advisedly, failed to take seriously a case brought by the Director of Public Prosecutions against the *Workers' Weekly* under the Incitement to Mutiny Act. The alleged offence was contained in an article urging British armed forces to refuse to engage in industrial disputes against their fellow workers. Seen by many as an attack on press freedom, the government case was further weakened by the arrest of the paper's deputy editor, who turned out to be a war veteran who had lost both feet in action. The uproar persuaded Hastings to withdraw the prosecution and to retire from politics. He returned to the bar while occupying his spare time as a dramatist.

The high point in a string of middle-ranking West End successes was *Scotch Mist*, which triumphed over hostile reviews (one critic called it 'the worst play I have ever seen') when the Bishop of London denounced the closing of the second act with the rape of the heroine, a role played by the alluringly sexy Tallulah Bankhead. For weeks there were queues at the box office.

With a vivacious wife, Hastings was a great party giver though if he was bored by his guests, he would disappear off to bed. Halfway through tea with Lady Hastings as the guest of King George V at Buckingham Palace, he startled the monarch with the words, 'Well, I must be off now, as I have some work to do.'

Patrick Hamilton began his descent into alcoholism in Albany. Success came early with his play *Rope*, written, as he told his brother Bruce, on scraps of paper in pubs and Lyons Corner House. This was to understate his achievement. He took enormous trouble with a plot based on a real case in which two young men plotted to commit the perfect murder.

> *The narrow, perverse genius of Rope is in its simplicity. At the front and centre of the stage is a chest which, we are soon told, contains the body of a recently murdered young man. Having set up this ghastly tableau, the murderers, and the playwright with them, can play sadistic variations, inviting the boy's father and sister to the flat, taking tea on the chest and so on. Hamilton had found an authentic addition to the repertoire of horror, without the employment of any on-stage violence or technical gimmickry.*

At age twenty-four, Hamilton had achieved fame so quickly and unexpectedly as to invite comparison with Noël Coward and with Lord Byron. The publication of a novel, *The Midnight Bell* (1929), immediately after the opening of *Rope* confirmed J.B. Priestley's opinion of Hamilton as 'one of the few serious young novelists in Britain'.

It was not enough. His brother noted signs of anxieties and heavy drinking.

After *Rope* came *Gaslight* (1938) another psychological thriller. Making, in his own words, 'an outstanding amount of money', Hamilton moved into Albany.

> *This may seem awfully extravagant but I have got in on the cheapest possible terms, and its being so central and quiet is really worth its weight in gold.*

Writing from experience, his most successful novel, *Hangover Square*, which turned on alcoholic excesses, was published in 1941. His drinking became more frequent and a good deal heavier. By the end of the war, he was reckoned to be drinking the equivalent of three bottles of whisky a day. Somehow he held off the grim reaper until 1962.

The prize for flamboyance went to Peter Coats, garden designer and gardening editor of the journal *House and Garden*. Coats floated about Albany in a white linen suit, a brightly coloured silk scarf and an ancient Panama hat. The lover of socialite politician and super snob, Chips Channon, he was the immediate cause of the breakup of Channon's marriage though this was not hard to bring about. While his design talent was widely admired, those close to him could tire easily of his bitchy superiority.

For admission to Albany, a family connection came in handy. The maverick MP Alan Clark was lucky on two counts. His father, the eminent art critic Lord Clark, not only owned an apartment but since it was little used, he was happy to assign it to his son as his London base.

'I am absolutely delighted you are prepared to try sharing it with me,' he wrote. 'It is such a marvellous property and I would hate to see it pass out of the family,' adding, 'It is convenient and will save you money.'

News of Alan Clark moving in was not welcomed by the trustees. Sometime earlier the Clark's apartment had been let on a short lease to Alan's friend, the idiosyncratic publisher, Anthony Blond. Wild parties with girls staying overnight upset other residents and brought down the wrath of the Secretary. Captain Evans, who had been in place since 1930 and was of an old-fashioned caste of mind (Blond described him as sour), protested in vain.

With Alan Clark returning on a permanent basis, the trustees feared more of the same. In the event, embarrassment for Albany came not so much by riotous living as by association with Clark's extramarital escapades. With the publication of his *Diaries* in 1983, came the revelation that Albany had been the scene of a triple seduction, a mother and two daughters, though not, as it happened, simultaneously. The identity of what Clark referred to as 'the coven' was revealed by Max Clifford, a none-too-scrupulous publicist who, acting for the supposedly aggrieved family, sold their story to the press. It became a two week sensation. Clark tried laughing it off. 'I probably have a different sense of morality to most people. I have changed my ways and am a reformed character now.' The reaction of the Albany trustees goes unrecorded.

William Stone, the lifelong champion of Albany and the owner of a fair portion of it, died in 1958, following his 101st birthday. Even after his demise he did not cease to amaze. Eyebrows were raised when it was revealed that he collected women's jewellery. 'Who wore the tiara?' asked a newspaper. The rhetorical question was raised again when the showpiece in question sold at auction for £2,100 (£45,000 today).

Another surprise came with the announcement that Stone had left his entire estate to Peterhouse, his Cambridge college. Challenged by a dismayed family, a four year legal battle ended in victory for Peterhouse. A severely functional accommodation student block was built in memory of William Stone, Squire of Piccadilly.

In the last half century, as property prices have risen precipitously, Albany has attracted fame and fortune. The roll call of Albanians include former prime minister Edward Heath (and for a short time, Margaret Thatcher), playwright Terence Rattigan, actor Terence Stamp, explorer and writer Bruce Chatwin, philosopher Sir Isaiah Berlin, photographer Lord Snowdon, decorator David Hicks and the art historian John Richardson who, as a long term resident, described Albany as a 'tranquil haven in the dead heart of London'.

Anecdotes of Albany singularity continue to surface. In a recent biography of Graham Greene, we learn that during his time in Albany the great writer was given to standing for hours on Piccadilly jotting down the numbers on the licence plates of passing cars.

# Epilogue

The challenge of writing about Piccadilly is knowing where to stop. Inevitably, there is an overlap with St James's on one side and with Soho on the other, both with rich, albeit contrasting histories. But Piccadilly has its own unique flavour. Though flowersellers have long since gone, the magnetic pull of Eros attracts daily crowds of sightseers and happy idlers.

What they see around them is recognisable from photographs of fifty or even a hundred years ago. Thankfully, the town planners, inspired by le Corbusier and brutalist architects, have retreated to the side lines. Though property developers still get away with erecting soulless blocks of flats and offices, the old iconic buildings stand out majestically as a reproof against the tawdry and second rate. While the famous Piccadilly lights are now restricted to a single giant screen, sacrificing charm to technological wizardry, the change has allowed more of the Circus to emerge from behind the bill boards.

Eros, the crowd-puller of Piccadilly

With the car having been deposed king of the urban street, the interests of pedestrians have taken priority and Piccadilly has become more pedestrian friendly. Now that one side of the Circus has been closed to traffic, the hope must be of banning the vehicles that clog the entry to Shaftesbury Avenue.

As for those who have carved their names on Piccadilly, we can only wonder what they would make of it all. Perhaps it is enough that they have now left their mark with life stories that amaze, amuse and, just occasionally, inspire.

# Bibliography

*Albany* in *Survey of London*. Vols. 31 and 32. St James, Westminster

Lady Clodagh Anson, *Victorian Days*. 1907

Brenda Assael, *The London Restaurant 1840-1914*. 2018

Clifford Bax, *Evenings in Albany*. 1942

John Betjeman, *Vintage London*. 1942

Marcus Binney, *The Ritz Hotel*. 1999

Sheila Birkenhead, Peace in Piccadilly, 1958

J.B. Booth, *London Town*. 1929; *Palmy Days*. 1957

Colin Brown, *Lady M*. 2018

Lord David Cecil, *The Young Melbourne*. 1939

*Chambers Journal of Popular Literature*. July 2nd, 1892

Matt Cook, *London and the Culture of Homosexuality*. 2003

J. Mordaunt Crook, *The Rise of Nouveaux Riches*. 1999

Arthur Irwin Dasent, *Piccadilly in Three Centuries*. 1920

Guy Deghy and Keith Waterhouse, *Ninety Years of Bohemia*. 1955

Guy Deghy *Paradise in the Strand. The Story of Romanos*. 1958

# Bibliography

Simon Dewes, *Piccadilly Pageant*. 1951

Michael Diamond, *Victorian Sensation*. 2003

M. Willson Disher, *Winkles and Champagne*. 1938

Francis Donaldson, *The Actor Managers*. 1970

Bryan Forbes, *Ned's Girl*. 1977

Amanda Foreman, *Georgiana, Duchess of Devonshire*. 1998

Sean French, *Patrick Hamilton. A Life*. 1993

Roger Fulford, *Hanover to Windsor*. 1960

Harry Furniss, *Paradise in Piccadilly*. 1925

Brian Gardner, *Mafeking. A Victorian Legend*. 1968

Richard Greene, *Russian Roulette: The Life and Times of Graham Greene*. 2020

Edna Healey, *Lady Unknown. The Life of Angela Burdett-Coutts*. 1978

Philip Henderson, *The Gay Sixties. The Saturday Book*. 1959

Christopher Hibbert, *Wellington: A Personal History*. 1997

Seymour Hicks, *Vintage Years*. 1940

Edward Knoblock, *Round the Room*. 1939

Osbert Lancaster, *Home Sweet Homes*. 1939

James Lees-Milne, *Another Self*. 1970

Malcolm Letts, *How the Foreigners Saw Us*. 1935

W. Macqueen-Pope, *Twenty Shillings in the Pound*. 1948; *Goodbye Piccadilly*. 1960

Jasper Maskelyne, *White Magic*. 1936

Rohan McWilliam, *London's West End*. 2020

Leslie Mitchell, *Bulwer Lytton, The Rise and Fall of a Victorian Man of Letters*. 2003

Martin Monico, *Notes for a Family History*. 2014; Private publication

John Morley, *Life of Gladstone*, Vol. I. 1908.

Ian Nairn, *Nairn's London*. 1966

Ralph Nevill, *Piccadilly to Pall Mall*. 1908; *London Clubs*. 1911

Lt. Col. Newnham-Davis, *Dinner and Diners. Where and How to Dine in London*. 1899

Sam Osmond, *William Stone of Peterhouse and Albany*. 2018

Ronald Pearsall, *The Worm in the Bud*. 1969

Hesketh Pearson, *Beerbohm Tree; his life and laughter*. 1956

Roy Porter, *London, A Social History*. 1994

Roland Quinault, *Gladstone and Slavery*. The Historical Journal, 52, 2 (2009)

James Ralph, *Critical Survey of Public Buildings,* 1728

Marie-Louise Ritz, *César Ritz*. 1938

Max Schlesinger, *Saunterings In and About London*. 1852

Donald Shaw, *London in the Sixties*. 1908

Vivian Stuart, *The Beloved Little Admiral*. 1967

A.J.P. Taylor, *Essays in English History*. 1977

Adolphe and John Thomson, *Street Life in London*. 1876

Ion Trewin, *Alan Clark. The Biography*. 2009

David Wainwright, *The British Tradition:. Simpson – a World of Style*. 1996

Jehanne Wake, *Sisters of Fortune*. 2010

Maureen Waller, *London 1945*. 2004

Gavin Weightman, Steve Humphries, *The Making of London 1914-1939*. 1984

T.H. White, *The Age of Scandal.* 1950

Frederick Willis, *101 Jubilee Road.* 1948

Franco Zeffirelli, *An Autobiography.* 1986

# Acknowledgements

Foremost my thanks to Richard Charkin for welcoming me to Mensch, his latest publishing venture. For many years Richard rode the high tide of publishing, as CEO of Macmillan and latterly of Bloomsbury.

Researching Piccadilly gave me many happy and constructive hours in the London Library, that superlative subscription library in St James's Square where the professionalism of an ever-supportive staff is one of the marvels of literary life.

My thanks also to Jill Fenner, my one-time PA, for helping to make sense of jumbled sentences and otherwise impenetrable notes and to my agent Michael Alcock, ever the wise and sympathetic counsellor.

Above all, I owe a huge debt to my wife Mary Fulton who keeps me up to the mark by pointing out textual sins of omission and commission.

I dedicate this book to my young grandchildren, Eve, Freya, Max, Leo and Aksel in the hope that their London will prove to be a voyage of exciting discovery.

# A Note on the Author

Barry Turner is an author, editor and reviewer. He has written thirty books including biographies and social history. As founding editor of The Writer's Handbook he took this annual reference title through to its twenty-fourth edition. He was editor of The Statesman's Yearbook from 1997 to 2014. He was a founder member and former chairman of the National Academy of Writing. He reviews classic crime for the Daily Mail. Barry lives in London and South West France.

Milton Keynes UK
Ingram Content Group UK Ltd.
UKHW040726010823
426141UK00004B/195